Between *You* and *Me*

Edited by GUSTAVE L. WEINSS

BY THE EDITOR

Fill Your Storehouse Right

At the end of every day, you are either richer or poorer, whether it be in money, in experience, or in knowledge. You cannot remain the same even if you want to, for always there is change.

But you can always strive to control the way in which changing conditions affect you by filling up your storehouse right.

You can accumulate money by systematic saving, and such a plan is good, for a storehouse of available funds does much to induce peace of mind.

You can profit by your experiences, sifting the good from the bad, and thus fill your storehouse with good counsel. "Experience is a good teacher," says the philosopher, "for it will help us to shape our future."

You can fill your storehouse with knowledge. Knowledge is a thing that cannot be readily taken away from us, and it can be increased continuously with very little effort.

So, "Would you be safely on your way? Then lay up treasures day by day." Save wisely; profit by your experiences; but, most of all, cram your storehouse full of knowledge, for knowledge will serve you well should "riches take wings and fly and leave you with a face awry."

□

The Joy of Doing Things

Of all the joys that enter into our lives, it would be difficult to find one greater than that which brings from us the exclamation, "See, I did this all myself."

Can you picture the delight that comes to a child who has mastered the art of writing his own name for the first time? Can you conceive the joyful assurance that thrills the inventor who has perfected the plan of his dreams?

You can, because you know yourself the joy that comes to you when you accomplish something you have set out to do. And be this something great or be it small, the joy that results from doing it is what makes life worth while because it arouses in us enthusiasm for greater things.

I know of a woman who, until about a year ago, could not bake a loaf of bread. And well do I know the happiness that came to her—and her family, too —when she tried and persisted and found out that she could make bread as well as the next person. Her achievement meant not only good home-made bread, and then cakes and pies for her family, but a mother filled with an inward glow of happiness and satisfaction in being able to do something she could not do before, a mother made more self-reliant with the assurance that she could do what she set out to do.

Yes, joy does come from discovering that we can do things, and it is the actual doing of them day by day that leads to worth-while accomplishments.

The daily performance of simple tasks closely akin to drudgery fits us for the performance of more important work without our being conscious of it. The making of a common apron, a simple waist or dress, a plain hat, besides affording joy in accomplishment at the time, produces in us the skill needed for making more elaborate wearing apparel. Even the studying of a lesson or a section or a single paragraph will enable us to claim for ourselves a bit of knowledge that we did not possess before.

Every greater act we perform is but the result of a lesser beginning. And our reward is not alone the joy that comes with doing things, but also the assurance, the confidence, we gain in our very selves.

□

The Secret of "Bigness"

Would you like to know the secret of being really "big"—not physically, but mentally? You can learn it if you are willing to carry out the resolutions offered by Dr. Frank Crane, but not if you merely read them:

"Just for today, I will exercise my soul in three ways, to wit:

"I will do somebody a good turn and not get found out. If anybody knows it, it will not count.

"I will do at least two things I don't want to do, as William James suggests, just for exercise.

"I will not show any one that my feelings are hurt. They may be hurt, but today I will not show it."

After you have tried this plan and learned the secret, put it into use as often as you can. It will do you no good merely to know it. As is true of all knowledge you acquire, you must continually put it into practice if you wish to profit by it.

Today's Dress—and Yesterday's

Mrs. Picken recently gave this instructive talk to an interested audience of women. We are passing it along to our readers, in order that they, too, may have the benefit of it.
—EDITOR.

By MARY BROOKS PICKEN
Director of Instruction

IN comparing today's dress with that of yesterday, I cannot help but remember the incident when, as a youngster, I, in fun, donned a corset and with smart grownupness paraded about in it. I was immediately sat down and told a very ugly, gruesome story about a woman who laced her corsets until her waist measured but 17 inches.

The story was to the effect that this woman, when she planned to go anywhere, even to church, would refrain from eating for two whole days; that when meal time came she would lace up her corsets to overcome her hunger; that they found her ribs had pressed themselves into her liver and had also crowded her stomach until the pain produced lockjaw and death when she was only thirty-one.

No skeleton in the night, no hoot owl or crying cat, ever put as much fear in my thought as did this story about the fatal effect of corsets. But as I came into womanhood and the story dimmed in my memory, vanity and apparent necessity put me into a corset at a time, fortunately for me, when the small waist had stretched itself into one of normalcy.

BUT before we pass on from the thought of the very small waist and tight corsets, I want to ask how many of you know that it is all a mistake about corsets originating in the 11th century? Egyptian mummies have been unearthed, which show that bandages as corsets existed more than 6,000 years ago. Corsets did, however, experience a great revival in the 11th century, and, as you know, 'twas Catherine de Medici two centuries later who made them famous, demanding, as she did, that all women of good birth and breeding in her kingdom reduce their waists to 13 inches. This was accomplished by many through great sacrifice, starvation, and pain, for to do it they had to wear a steel corset of armor plate that was torturous in every sense.

I wish time permitted—I'd like so to tell you of the first corsets of bandages; then of the ones of ¼-inch skins punctured with holes; then of the armor-plate ones that I have just mentioned, the wearing of which could only produce tittering, silly women, made hysterical, I would say, from the very aching of their bodies.

EVER since the 13-inch waist spree, moralists and physicians and many other good citizens have decried the use of corsets. How much credit is due to these people for their work and how much is due to the progress and independence of women in the present day, are in themselves subjects for a whole evening. At any rate, we should realize that the present state is one of growth. Also, we should appreciate what it signifies for the future.

Corsets have three functions—only two if slenderness is the asset and exercise and much walking are the habit. These are, respectively, to hold up the stockings and to make for a neat waist line. The third reason—you all know it already—is that a corset helps to confine the hips and to control a surplus of flesh. Women everywhere realize that a corset should be worn for neatness and not for support. A back that cries for a corset needs, instead, waist and back exercises that will overcome the sense of fatigue when a corset is not worn.

I READ the other day that an old man goes through a business depression much better than a young man because the older man knows that when a panic has subsided conditions will be more nearly normal and better than for several years, and so he endures the depression for the sake of the good times that, from experience, he knows are coming.

And those of you who have followed the evolution of women's clothes realize with me that we are approaching, if not experiencing, a period where the modest woman's dress, even if not artistic, is the sanest, healthiest, and most natural of all periods.

To prove this, look back at your grandmother and your mother and the clothes they wore—tight corsets, garters, long germ-trailing skirts, many petticoats, high collars, and sometimes big, stiff sleeves.

I have heard a good old man tell, in teasing his wife, that when he courted her, when he took her to church, there was not room in the buggy for her, her sleeves, and him, so he was forced to walk alongside and drive.

THE disappearance of the high collar has made it possible for us to pry into our neighbor's business without so much discomfort, and, besides, doctors say that throat troubles are reduced to half what they were and we know that necks have no ugly brown lines from restricted circulation. Some say, in defense of the high collar, "Yes, but look at the double chin." But doctors say that such chins are not health hampering and we who have them know that they are most comfortable.

The soft, cozily warm coat of today is another expression of good sense and health in clothes. All of you remember when the modish Christy girl donned a thin suit, a fur neck piece, black patent-leather pumps, silk stockings, white kid gloves, and a violet corsage, and faced the bitterest winter weather, feeling that she was beautifully and properly attired. The coat has done away with the thin suit in winter. The one-piece dress has replaced, almost entirely, the thin shirtwaist in business and has given us at least garments with weight carried on the shoulders, rather than at the waist line. High-heeled shoes are tottering out, and arctics, ugly as they are, even when properly buckled, are, in blustering winter, making amends for the absence of high shoes.

HATS without hat pins are another evidence of growth. The crown of a hat, to be rightly proportioned, should be large enough to fit the head, but we have been a long time getting our heads to a right size to fit our hats. Still, that has been accomplished and few of us can believe that we will ever go back to the little hat pinned on the topmost top of our heads.

We have had for a time the extreme in short skirts, but they are passing with the "flappers." All Paris is talking slightly longer skirts. Already they have found favor in America. Plucked eyebrows are no longer fashionable. Bobbed hair is being tucked under. Rouge is growing paler with the days, and so the flapper and the modish, modest woman are keeping step just now.

A FASHION authority of international reputation has written pages about the "shackles of dress," saying that women could never make a success in business because of the length of time consumed in putting on and taking off and in caring for their clothing.

The time was when women could not have done one other thing but dress and preside or chatter as the occasion demanded. But that isn't true today. Some of the brightest, most capable, and happiest women I know dress in beautifully becoming good taste and yet dress and undress as quickly as any man. The fates evened things up for man and woman when they gave hair to be dressed to a woman and beards to be shaved to a man; so, with those handicaps, an even start is assured, and with present-day fashions no woman need take more time for her toilette than her husband or brother.

When we women look back, we must glory in the common sense that has been brought to bear in women's dress. We truly have occasion to be glad and grateful.

Today's materials are beautiful; shoes are smart and comfortable. You can sing or run a race in your corsets; hats stay on and stockings stay up. And since we can actually get dressed before breakfast, we should be glad, for we can see that efficiency has dawned on the horizon of women's dress. Now, to work, to make modern dress beautiful, and we shall have perfection.

Fabric *Dominates* Spring Millinery

By MARY MAHON
Department of Millinery

THE use of such fabrics as all-over visca, timbo, cellophane, "triple" taffeta, Canton crêpe, moiré, and faille is an outstanding characteristic in the styling of hats for early spring. There is an infinite variety of these different fabrics and they assume the most fanciful arrangements. Usually they come in the popular laque effect, which, by the way, is the new term for ciré and means the same polished or glacé finish.

Shapes and colors are next in importance, because when fanciful fabrics are employed in developing hats, elaborate trimmings are dispensed with, and the hat beautiful depends on the line, angle, or flare of the shape, features that are very much in evidence at present, together with the color or the combination of colors that is most becoming to the wearer.

TWO charming hats of faultlessly artistic contour are illustrated in the cover design of this issue of INSPIRATION. The one at the left, an effective combination of Newport green, black, and white, is presented in a medium-large, broad-at-the-side poke shape of timbo straw in the new shade of green that strongly resembles jade. The edge of the brim is finished with a tiny roll or tubular flange. The crown is shaped down in telescope effect at the back and sides, forming an even, light roll across the front, the base of it being finished with a tubular roll similar to that used on the edge. The flower trim, which is applied at the right side back, both on the top and the under brim, consists of several white pond lilies, the edges of the petals being tipped in black lacquer, and a spray of green foliage.

THE hat illustrated at the right emphasizes clearly that the broad-side, short-back, slightly mushroom brim, regardless of its minute or exaggerated proportions, is anchored in styledom. The variations that can be made with this type of brim as a basis are unlimited. In the development of this model, black visca all-over is used for the top brim and soft balloon crown, and black Canton crêpe makes the facing. The regularity of line and the somber blackness of this hat awaken no special interest until it is supplemented with two brilliant-green bead parrots that spread their long tails and wings flat over the front of the crown and on the side brim. These gaily colored bead and embroidery birds are new, and, in this country, they are used in preference to feathered birds, which are quite the mode in Paris.

WHAT is more suggestive of spring than the solid flowered turban or toque that sometimes widens out into picturesque tab extensions at each side? Equally interesting is the medium-sized upturned brim of flowers and fabric combination, shown at the upper left of this page. Violets provide a typical spring flower and color.

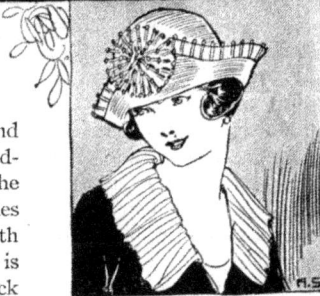

The foundation is a vizor-brim turban having a narrow coronet running across the front to each side and a wider one at the back which flares out in a wing effect at the sides. Purple visca braid is used to cover the back coronet and crown, the braid being sewed in strips from the head-size on top over the edge of the brim to the head-size underneath, and from the base of the crown up to the center top, an apex being formed by one strip of braid being lapped over the other. The front coronet is covered with a bias strip of silk-warp crêpe, and before it is stitched into the head-size on top, the violets are appliquéd on the outside. The inside facing is then stitched to the head-size and a band of narrow ribbon is drawn around the base of the crown.

CANNA visca develops the delightful wide-at-the-side model in the center. The brim, faced with self-toned taffeta, is made backless by a slash that runs into the head-size at the direct back and is then cut off so as to make a curve. The portion of the brim at the right side is left a little wider, so as to serve as a foundation for the flat roses that are appliquéd on this side and continued in a trifle on the under facing. A band of two-tone ribbon is drawn around the crown and finished with a bow at the left side front.

TIGER-LILY color, which closely resembles the established old rose shade of yore, combined with a wreath of tiny black cherries and long, pointed, green glacéd leaves as a trimming, is the color scheme of the model at the right. A medium-sized cloche shape with a rather large bell crown is fitted plain with faille, the under facing being made of a plateau in the same shade, only a little darker in tone. The wreath of cherries and foliage encircles the base of the crown, and, at the right side back, where the edge of the brim is turned under toward the head-size, a large bunch of the foliage and cherries, tied with a piece of black velvet ribbon, is attached, one long end of the ribbon falling over the right shoulder.

ORNAMENTS are of surpassing interest this season owing to the extreme novelty in their design, and the success of the new hats is insured by the use of these ornate trimmings.

Among the genuinely new effects in ornaments is the Etain cabochon, which in reality is ordinary tinfoil crumpled over a buckram foundation, with mother-of-pearl embroidered in the folds. The idea is rather novel; nevertheless, it is meeting with favor and is extremely effective on large, dark-colored moiré hats with irregular brim tendencies.

"Fire cracker" is indeed an appropriate name for the attractive model at the lower center, which is developed of Batavia cloth in feu Lanru, a new flame red. Its upturned brim is flanged by a row of red match-stick beads tipped with tiny steel beads. The brim forms a diadem in the front, and a huge rosette or pompon of the beads is applied at the point. In some instances, long wooden beads are shellacked and colored to look like galilith or ivory, and when tipped with a steel bead they make an effective trim for an all-black hat.

The foundation frame for this model is the regulation chin-chin brim with a medium high round crown. This foundation is first covered with flame-color, silk-warp crêpe. The top brim and crown are then covered plain with Batavia, the outside or facing of the brim being applied in two sections, or flanges. The first one, which is about 1 inch wide, is applied at the edge, and then the row of match sticks, which come in a fringe, is applied on this flange, the steel beads at the top being allowed to extend beyond the edge. The remaining portion of the brim covering is applied next. This finishes the raw edge of the flange and match-stick trimming by means of a corded edge. Then the brim is shaped into the crown at the center front, and the rosette made of myriads of the little spikes is applied in the dented portion. Sequins that are shaped long and pointed, after the manner of a blade of grass, are also used for this type of trimming or for the entire facing.

The *Well-Stocked* Linen Closet

By ALWILDA FELLOWS
Department of Dressmaking

FEW modern brides-to-be are absorbed in the preparation of household linens to the extent of devoting hours and hours to very fine, tedious handwork, for the business and social activities of the average girl take up such a large portion of the day and evening that there is but little time left for any other than the very necessary sewing and dressmaking.

In spite of this, the modern linen chest holds its own very well in comparison with the chest of former years. The little it has lost in the lack of fine handwork done by its possessor seems to be more than made up by her quickly executed but nevertheless very effective embroidery of the kind that is now so popular, and also by the exquisite bits of foreign needlework that are really not prohibitive as to price.

Several examples of the kind of embroidery that so quickly and delightfully stocks the present-day linen chest are shown on this page.

FIRST of all, illustrated at the left, is a set of containers not only for linens, but for the choice silverware that one may desire to keep from becoming scratched or from tarnishing when it is not in use. The set is made in tan cotton of a rather coarse weave similar to linen and is decorated with appliqué in the form of patches of chambray in various colors secured in position by short blanket-stitches of the same color as the chambray. An enlarged detail of the appliqué is shown just above the set. The edges of the set are blanket-stitched in a medium, rather bright blue, and the lettering is outlined in the same color.

For the knife container, supply a piece of material 20 inches long and 24 inches wide and, if you wish to interline the casing portion, a piece of light-weight Canton flannel 17 inches long and 18 inches wide. To make the container, apply the Canton flannel as a facing with one of its corners even with the lower right-hand corner of the material, thus leaving an extension of the material at the left and above the Canton flannel. Then fold the faced portion lengthwise through the center,

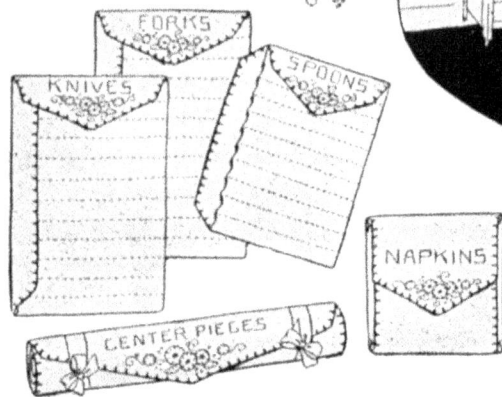

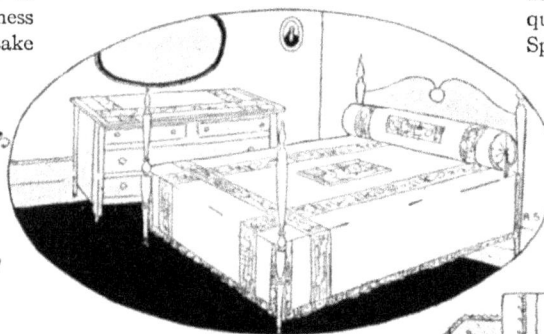

mark the lines for the casings, usually a dozen, and stitch through the four thicknesses of the material on the marked lines. Afterwards, shape the extensions at the left and at the top as you desire them and apply the decorations. The extension at the left will form a flap that may be folded back over the openings, and the one at the top a flap to indicate the contents of the container after it is rolled up. To hold the roll, apply tapes or tie a ribbon around it.

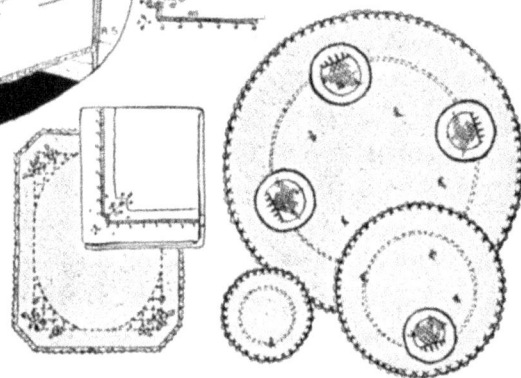

Make the fork and spoon containers in a similar manner, using a piece of material 18 inches wide for teaspoons and 24 inches wide for soup spoons or tablespoons.

A cardboard foundation such as may be obtained in an art needlework shop or department is required for the center-piece roll. This may be of any size you desire.

For the napkin case, provide a piece of material 24 inches square and from each corner of this cut out 8-inch squares, thus leaving strips long enough to fold over a dozen dinner napkins folded in the regulation manner.

LUNCHEON SETS are shown in such a charming variety of outline, materials, and decorations that it is difficult to make a selection. Ecru, or natural, linen is now popular in both plain and damask weaves.

At the extreme right are shown the center piece and a plate and a tumbler doily of an ecru-linen luncheon set that is edged with cross-stitched hems and embroidered in soft rose, blue, and green in darning-, blanket-, and cross-stitches.

Next to the set of doilies is a white luncheon cloth embroidered in the vivid peasant colorings now so popular. An enlarged detail of the embroidery, which is in darning- and fine blanket-stitch effect, is shown above it.

Underneath the luncheon cloth is shown one of a set of doilies in ecru linen edged with a rather coarse ecru lace and embroidered in blue, canna, and black in darning- and lazy-daisy-stitches. It is not possible to obtain transfer patterns for the embroidery designs, but you will have no difficulty in copying them.

BED COVERINGS are a very important part of the linen-chest equipment nowadays, but those of an unusual nature are quite expensive if purchased ready made. Spreads of unbleached muslin with large appliqué designs in color or designs in tufted, or coarse French-knot, effect can be made very quickly at a minimum expense. Or, if a spread of finer quality is desired, this may be made of marquisette of substantial weave, beach cloth, or jewel cloth, which is a rather coarse plain weave with open work that forms a check effect, and trimmed with insertion.

At the upper center is shown a spread with bolster cover to match, trimmed very attractively with strips of filet insertion and filet pieces. Dresser, dressing-table, and chifforobe covers to match would make an unusually lovely bedroom set.

THE requirements of a linen chest vary according to the size of the prospective home and the amount of entertaining that will probably be done. Dining-room linens usually should include from three to six table cloths, one of large size with 1 dozen dinner napkins to match, 1 dozen napkins for ordinary use, one or more luncheon sets, and as many buffet covers, center pieces, and doilies for various purposes as one's time and linen allowance will permit.

Kitchen linens should include at least a dozen dish towels and as many dish cloths.

Bedroom linens should be regulated in quantity by the number of bedrooms. As a rule, 1 dozen sheets, 1 to 1½ dozen pillow slips, three or four bed spreads, three blankets, three comfortables, and three or four sets of covers for the dressers, etc., are ample for two bedrooms.

For the bathroom, an abundance of linens are required. At least 1 dozen towels for ordinary use, ½ to 1 dozen bath towels, ½ to 1 dozen guest towels, 1 dozen wash cloths, and one or two bath mats are none too many.

The fastidious taste calls for initials or monograms on table and bed linens. Although not essential, such work gives an individuality that is very desirable and, besides, simple initials do not require a great deal of time for their development.

Perfecting the Woman's Workshop

By LAURA MacFARLANE
Editorial Department

WE have been hearing a great deal about efficiency during the last ten years. And what has been the result? A marked improvement in the running of business concerns, in the working of farms, in the making of automobiles—in fact, every line of endeavor has shown an upward tendency.

But can we say the same thing of the running of the home—the domain over which the housewife presides? Much has been accomplished by the home economics departments of schools, colleges, and magazines, but there is no business today that has been so backward in adopting up-to-date methods and the findings of science as that of housekeeping. How many kitchens do you see that are equipped with the same devices that the housewife's mother and grandmother used? A great many, I'll wager. And all because we hesitate to take advantage of the improved devices that manufacturers are perfecting for us and we are slow to adopt the short-cuts in modern cookery methods that experts in home management are showing us all the time.

Instead of making so brave an attempt to furnish living rooms, reception halls, and bedrooms so that they will be admired by your friends, why not resolve to expend the same energy and money on the kitchen with the thought that this room—your workshop—must be your most interesting room, since it is here that you carry on the engineering of your home? Then it will become a pleasant spot and the usual drudgery of housework will lose its sting. And the best part of this plan is that your vitality will be saved for the more esthetic aspects of life, which are conducive not only to growth and development but to happiness and contentment as well.

IN ORDER to overcome guesswork in baking and roasting and the cooking failures that are likely to result, your stove should contain an oven thermometer. In the latest gas-stove models, the oven, which has a glass door, is placed at the side so as to prevent the inevitable stooping that the older kinds require. Also, mechanical devices that regulate the temperature are now installed in stoves so that food left in the oven while one goes out for the afternoon will be cooked to a turn upon one's return. There are, too, combination stoves which burn both coal and gas or electricity, thus permitting the use of whatever fuel is most convenient. Hot-water heaters make it possible to have hot water at all times. If a fireless cooker is used, see to it that it is raised from the floor either in its construction or by means of an additional stand.

If the home is wired for electricity, you may take advantage of the numerous electrical devices for cooking that the market boasts. The electric toaster, grill, waffle iron, griddle, percolator, all permit cooking at the table and naturally encourage conversation and good feeling. And the mere mention of electricity brings to our minds numberless household devices for eliminating fatigue in housework—the vacuum cleaner, the electric washer, the electric iron, the motor dish washer, the electric ice-cream freezer, to say nothing of mayonnaise mixers and related utensils. Yes, "chained lightning" has already overcome much of the drudgery of housework and is constantly exploring new fields.

WHEN you investigate a sink, you should give the most thought to its height from the floor and its design, for practically every one has now been converted to the sanitary type of sink made out of porcelain, enameled iron, or vitreous china. The backache caused by constantly bending over a sink that is not installed at just the right height for the worker, is familiar to most housewives. If you are over 5 feet tall, your sink should be at least 35 inches from the floor, and higher still if your height runs about 5 feet 6 inches. The correct height can be determined very easily by experiment.

The sink with the double drain board is the most efficient kind. Then the soiled dishes can be piled on one drain board—the right usually—washed, and placed on the other, thus overcoming waste motion and preventing the breakage that often results if the dishes are piled in the sink. The mixing faucet shown at the center top of the illustration makes it possible to have water at whatever temperature is desired.

SEVERAL details in the kitchen table increase its efficiency. It should be on rollers so as to be easily moved and its top should be made of enamel or zinc, so that hot dishes may be set on it without disastrous results. If your kitchen is of a size to permit it, a table such as shown in the upper left-hand corner will prove an inestimable help. Here a shelf under the table takes care of many of the large cooking utensils and the center rack over the table holds others, as well as contains hooks for those that can be hung. And drawers for knives, etc. are also a feature. Imagine the joy of preparing a meal with practically every one of your utensils within arm's reach.

Too much cannot be said about the kitchen cabinet. There can be no excuse for not having everything in its place when there is a place provided for everything. How much more you can enjoy your afternoon callers if you have not exhausted your energy and your patience by making countless trips to the pantry for the flour, the nutmeg, the vanilla, etc. when you are making the dainty cakes to serve them. A kitchen cabinet also provides an additional working surface and height, certain types of work requiring one height, and certain others, another.

When you are selecting a work chair for your kitchen, choose one that is at least 15 inches higher than the usual chair. And make sure that it has a back, as here shown,

Double-lipped saucepans permit pouring from either side.

A teakettle with double boiler eliminates an extra utensil.

A rolling pin containing ice makes good pastry-making simple.

A flexible spatula is always in demand.

A long-handled spoon removes the contents from tall bottles.

A set of measuring spoons prevents uncertain measurements.

An apple corer removes the cores of apples with rapidity.

A lemon squeezer with place for contents prevents waste.

Wire whips can be had with meshes of any size.

A potato ricer easily wins over the old-time potato masher.

ALICE SEIPP

Continued on page 8

Continued from page 7

to prevent fatigue. A small step-ladder is a very useful thing in a kitchen and it provides an extra seat. A wheel cart with removable tray, as shown in the upper right-hand corner, makes it possible to carry all the soiled dishes from the table in one trip and facilitates numerous other tasks.

MUCH more could be said about the kitchen efficient—the various kinds of floor coverings, the correct arrangement of the kitchen equipment, the caring of the refrigerator, the advisability of keeping a household file, etc. —but all these are big matters in themselves. Shall we just mention the kitchen beautiful and let it go at that?

Have you ever gone into a kitchen in which the windows were so placed as to admit the streaming sunlight and were curtained with dainty checked gingham, the walls were a pretty tan and the floor a soft green or blue, where a snow-white sink held sway on one side and a white enameled stove on the other, with a white kitchen cabinet in between, where gleaming aluminum pans hung like mirrors in stately rows—in fact, a kitchen in which pretty colors harmonized and every article of furniture seemed to be chosen with an eye for beauty as well as utility? If you have, then you know the desire and inspiration it gave you to revolutionize your kitchen at home; if you haven't, why not resolve to make your own kitchen one of which you will be proud and in which you will find pleasure in performing even the homeliest tasks?

Woman's Institute *Question Box*

Making Wide-Sleeve Pattern

Will you please give instructions for making a pattern for the new wide sleeves that have a very long armhole line and, also, tell how to change the armhole of the waist pattern to correspond?　P. W.

The most satisfactory method of developing these patterns is to use as a foundation a kimono waist pattern made with a very deep effect at the armhole, place this on the figure, and mark on it the position you desire the armhole line. To form the separate waist and sleeve patterns, cut the kimono pattern on the marked line. Before you use the pattern for a garment, it will be well for you to try this out in muslin to make sure that the line is correct.

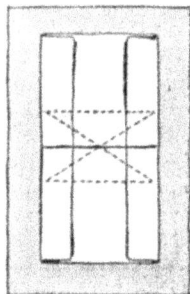

FIG. 1

A Simple Bound Buttonhole

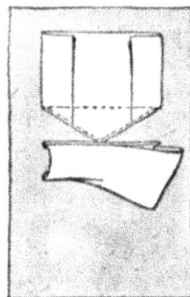

FIG. 2

For the idea of making a bound buttonhole in the very simple manner that is here illustrated, we are indebted to Mr. Edmund Gurney, who conducts classes in tailoring in the University of California and the Oregon Agriculture College. Mr. Gurney very kindly gave us permission to pass this idea on to Woman's Institute students.

This method is suitable for making buttonholes in wash and silk fabrics and for silk-bound buttonholes in woolen fabrics. For each buttonhole, provide a straight piece of self-fabric or contrasting fabric $\frac{1}{2}$ inch wider than you wish the buttonhole and about $2\frac{1}{2}$ inches long. Turn under each of the long

FIG. 3

edges of the strip $\frac{1}{4}$ inch and press them flat; then place the strip, as shown in Fig. 1, so that its crosswise center is directly over the line marked for the buttonhole and its sides are even with the ends of this line.

With the strip pinned or basted to the dress, stitch in the manner indicated by the dotted lines, diagonally through the center in opposite directions and straight across the strip, about $\frac{1}{4}$ inch above and below the crosswise center. Then slash along the crosswise center on the heavy line just to the turned edges of the strip, cutting through the dress material as well as the binding strip and being very careful not to extend the slash farther than the edges of the strip.

Next, cut away the surplus binding material close to the diagonal stitching, as shown in Fig. 2, draw the free ends of the strip through the opening to the wrong side and press the strip back over the crosswise stitching. The illustration shows one free end drawn partly through the opening.

Finish the binding on the wrong side by turning under each raw edge and slipping it down over the lines of crosswise stitching, just as you would finish an ordinary binding. Then, with extremely fine stitches, whip down the turned edges at the ends on both the right and the wrong side, taking several stitches over the ends of the opening on the wrong side so as to prevent them from tearing out. Fig. 3 shows the finished buttonhole.

Want to Get Acquainted?

The following Institute students desire to become acquainted with other Institute students residing in their localities:

Millersburg, Pa. . . . . G. M. N.
Billings, Mont. . . . . L. C. D.
Springfield, Ohio . . . . L. D.
East St. Louis, Ill. . . . . E. G.
United States or foreign countries . . . . R. S.
New York, N. Y. . . . . M. A. P.
Orange or Newark, N. J. . . . . J. S. S.
Providence, R. I. . . . . K. A. L.
Atlantic City, N. J. . . . . E. W.
Donora, Pa. . . . . M. D. M.
Mt. Vernon, N. Y. . . . . S. W. S.
Chicago, Ill. . . . . M. S.
Centralia or Mt. Vernon, Ill. . . . . M. G.
Reading, Pa. . . . . R. N. G.
Massachusetts . . . . I. P. S.

I should like to become acquainted with a milliner, preferably in Kansas, who needs help in her shop.　E. B.

I should like to become acquainted with Institute students about 19 years of age.　G. K.

I should like to become acquainted with a Dressmaking student about 20 years of age who lives in Southern New York or Northeastern Pennsylvania.　H. B.

I should like to correspond with some one in the millinery business in Western Iowa or Eastern Nebraska who would like an honest, reliable partner.　S. M. W.

I should like to correspond with a student who desires to open a shop in the eastern part of Pennsylvania.　M. B. M.

I should like to get in touch with a good milliner in Illinois, Indiana, or Ohio who needs an assistant in her shop. I am a student in millinery and have almost completed the course.　L. McM.

I should like to get in touch with some one who has a small shop here in Brooklyn Heights, N. Y., and would like me to make things for her to sell.　H. B. H.

I should like to become acquainted with a married woman about 24 years of age who lives on a farm and would correspond with me.　G. A. O'D.

I should like to correspond with girl students of the Institute about 18 years of age.　M. H.

I should like to become acquainted with Institute students living in Boston or vicinity.
Miss Anna R. Skillin,
252 Marlborough St.,
Boston, Mass.

I should like to correspond with girls 16 or 17 years of age who are taking the Dressmaking and Tailoring Course.　H. F. K.

I should like to correspond with an Institute student living on a farm in Michigan who is from 18 to 20 years old and is taking the Dressmaking Course. V. G. B.

I should like to become acquainted with a Dressmaking student in Chicago, Ill., or vicinity. My telephone number is Rogers Park 6039—address 6401 Ridge Avenue.　J. L.

I should like to become acquainted with Dressmaking students in or near Redlands, Calif., who wish to form a club. Also, I should like to correspond with Spanish girls outside of Redlands. My telephone number is Blue 1036.　Miss Carmen Lopez,
1017 Calhoun St.,
Redlands, Calif.

I should like to become acquainted with Institute students about 21 years of age who live in Schenectady, Albany, or Saratoga, N. Y.　P. G.

I should like to correspond with Institute students in the vicinity of Girard, Ill.
Miss Mabel Perrine,
R. R. No. 2,
Girard, Ill.

I should like to become acquainted with girls 18 years of age living in the vicinity of Duluth, Minn., who are taking the Complete Dressmaking Course or the Millinery Course.　E. M. H.

I should like to become acquainted with a student of the Complete Dressmaking Course living in Anderson, Indianapolis, Tipton, Ind., or anywhere in that state, who has a shop and would like to have an assistant.　M. C.

I should like to become acquainted with a Millinery student in Toronto, Canada. My telephone number is Belmont 28.　C. W. H.

I should like to become acquainted with students of the Complete Dressmaking Course. My telephone number is 582R Bell Phone, Lancaster, Pa.　A. M. G.

I should like to correspond with Institute students in Missouri who would like to go into business or who desire help.　H. J. V.

I should like to correspond with a Dressmaking student living in Washington along the coast, preferably one who has a daughter 2 or 3 years old to dress.　E. M. S.

I should like to become acquainted with Institute students who are interested in opening a dressmaking shop with another student.　J. B.

I should like to correspond with some one in Elmira, Rochester, Geneva, or Syracuse, N. Y., particularly with one taking the Dressmaking or Millinery Course who might be interested in opening a shop for women's and children's things—lingerie, children's clothes, nurses, furnishings, negligées—not an ordinary dressmaking shop, but more in the line of a woman's exchange and made-to-order things. M. S.

If other Woman's Institute students would like to get in touch with the inquiring students, we shall be glad to supply the addresses that are not printed here.

Our Students' Own Page

How I Solved Our Clothes Problems

Nearly a year ago, before taking up the Dressmaking Course in the Woman's Institute, I didn't know how I was going to get the clothes that my children and I needed, and now our clothes are both beautiful and good.

Last spring the serge street dress I wanted was marked $40. I made one like it for $15 and made nicer sleeves and a prettier embroidery design. The nicest skirt I ever wore is a box-plaited plaid that cost me $5. The same skirt ready made would have cost from $12 to $15. I made some pretty blouses out of two of my last summer's dresses. My mother gave me two voile dresses of hers, one figured and one plain, the waists of both were worn, but the two skirts made me a beautiful summer dress, as they were both lavender shades and combined well.

I have made all the children's clothes out of what my sister had laid away as being worn out, but were perfectly good, only out of style.

I made myself some beautiful underwear. One silk petticoat would have cost me $7, and I made a set of four pieces for that.

I made all my husband's shirts for half what he used to pay for them, and they are made of better materials.

I intend copying a brown broadcloth suit that is marked $65 in a store window. The material and findings have cost me $20 and I can now have the proper shoes, gloves, and hat that go with a suit to make it perfect, and it will be the first nice suit I ever had.

I draft all my own patterns, which is a great saving, as I used to spend more in patterns than the garments I would make were worth. I can now put the simple new ideas into my dresses which the dressmakers here seem afraid to attempt.

When I told my husband that I had paid for everything we all needed and nearly paid for my Course out of my clothes-allowance money, he said I had done more than well and we had never looked better. But it is to the Woman's Institute I owe it all, for without its help I would never have been able to do the things I have done. Besides, I have learned something that will be a saving and a pleasure to me as long as I live.

Mrs. Effie M. Price,
Indian Head, Sask., Can.

Girls in College Admire Daughter's Clothes

All my life, or since I was old enough to want pretty, attractive clothes, I have wished and wished that I were a seamstress. There being a large family—ten of us—I was always lamenting about the high cost of living and especially our clothing bills. We could not afford expensive clothes nor very many, as five of us are women.

I had read so much about the Woman's Institute and its wonderful work that my husband was very eager for me to try the Course. He said, "Why not take up a Course; I am sure you will make a successful seamstress, if any one can."

I did not think I could learn by mail, but any one can, it is so simple and easy. I do all of my own housework and care for seven children. At night I spend two pleasant hours with the Woman's Institute; besides, I go out one or two nights a week or have company.

The Woman's Institute has taught me to use less material, to cut to better advantage, and to fit properly; and the alteration of patterns is wonderful. I have made thirty or forty dresses this summer, using the same plain-waist pattern for all. Some of them were elaborate organdies and taffetas, organdy and tissue ginghams combined, and two beautiful ones of taffeta and gingham combined. I have several orders for more. Every one was so pleased with them, and I had the best of results. I can copy expensive dresses for one-fourth of what they would cost ready made and use the best of materials.

My 16-year-old daughter, who attended Baylor College this summer, says the girls told her she had the daintiest and prettiest dresses there. She said she would be walking on the campus and a crowd of girls would pass and remark about her pretty dresses.

My husband is so proud of my sewing that he is always complimenting the things I make. "Thanks to the Woman's Institute." My only regrets are that I did not take up the Course sooner, because we not only save so much on our clothes, but now we have more and nicer ones.

The Institute has also brought a new happiness into our home. It is a joy and pleasure to plan and make a young girl's wardrobe. I am preparing my 19-year-old daughter for State. She is so proud of her dresses and has so many more than usual. I have taken old, partly worn-out dresses and clothes that were out of style and made beautiful new dresses. All the expense would be for trimming or something to combine with them. Two of the prettiest dresses were taffeta and tissue ginghams; one, a $24.50

model, I copied for $2.85, and the other, a $19.50 model, I made for $3.25, which was for 3 yards of gingham, buttons, and cord.

I am very anxious to complete the Dressmaking Course so I can start your Millinery Course. The Woman's Institute has been a great help and inspiration to all of us. We take better care of our clothes and are so proud of them. I learn new things daily and use the knowledge I have gained through the Institute every day, even in mending. I used to give away the old pants and coats, but now, by cleaning, pressing, and turning, make the little boys beautiful and serviceable trousers out of them.

Mrs. E. A. Sherrill,
Beaumont, Texas.

How I Increased Our Family Income

It had always been my desire to learn to do millinery work, but I had never had a chance to learn it until one day when, reading in a Butterick Quarterly, I noticed an advertisement of the Woman's Institute. I showed the ad to my husband, and after discussing the question awhile, it was decided that I should have a trial at learning what I wanted most to know.

So immediately I wrote for more detailed information. As a result, I very soon had my first three lessons and was so enthusiastic over them that I almost neglected my housework that I might study more.

I received my first lessons in March, 1920, and, thanks to the Institute, I haven't had to buy a single hat since, for with the knowledge gained from my first lesson and some ideas I got from Inspiration, I took an old hat that couldn't possibly have been worn again and some material that I had on hand and made myself the best looking little hat; and no one ever suspected that I had made the hat myself.

Thus my hat-making career began.

Next I made myself a maline hat just like one that I saw in a shop window. The material cost me only $5 and the model that I patterned from was priced $27.50.

Then I took some blue crêpe de Chine and made a hat for my little 5-year-old daughter.

A friend asked me where I got such a lovely little hat for my daughter, and when I told her that I made it myself she could hardly believe that I did. She then wanted one for each of her two little girls. She was so well pleased with the hats when I got them finished that she wanted me to make a hat for her.

After making those hats just a few words from her informed some of her friends about the work I could do, and I soon had orders to make all the hats that I had the time to make.

I thought it was the grandest thing I ever did when I had learned enough to make my own hats, because I very soon realized how much money I was saving; and as my husband's earnings are not large, I felt that I was helping him also. But when I began to make hats for others and collect real dollars, can you imagine my happiness in being able to add to our little bank account?

The Woman's Institute deserves and shall have the praise for all that I have done. I am now planning to make my own fall and winter hats from some material that I have had for a long time. Before I learned to make hats, I was wondering what I would ever do with these same materials, for then they were worthless to me.

Mrs. Belle Burton,
Ovalo, Texas.

Fashion Service

SUPPLEMENT

Each Issue of *Vintage Notions Monthly* includes a *Fashion Service Supplement*. You will read about the fashion styles popular in the early twentieth century and receive a collectible fashion illustration to print and frame.

The students of the Woman's Institute would also receive a publication called *Fashion Service*. Where the *Inspiration* newsletter instructed them on all aspects of the domestic arts, not only sewing but also cooking, housekeeping, decorating, etc., *Fashion Service* was devoted entirely to giving current fashions with a key to their development.

Fashion Service prided itself on providing it's readers with reliable style information and the newest fashion forecasting. The publication wasn't just eye candy. The Institute stressed the importance of studying the fashions to benefit the sewer's understanding of dressmaking. To quote founder Mary Brooks Picken, "Once the principles of design...and of construction... are understood, beautiful garments will result. This publication comes to you as an aid to this desired goal. Read the text of every page and reason out the why of every illustration and description that your comprehension of designing and construction may be enlarged and your appreciation made more acute."

Today, these articles and illustrations give us a historically accurate view of what fashion really meant 100 years ago. Not only can we study these articles for an "of-the-time" style snapshot, but just as their students did, we can also learn to understand the principles of design and increase our sewing skills. In each issue, look for a collectible illustration in the back of the supplement!

Springtime Fashions

The lovely woman of today has good taste, emphasizes charm, evidences poise. Her clothes express life, joy in the new, and appreciation of the old.

* * *

Such a woman reads, studies, observes, and knows for herself the smart new, the beautiful old, and what of the two she can wear with charm and distinction.

* * *

So lovely ladies everywhere, read, enjoy, and use to the fullest the Fashion and sewing hints given here. Remember, in your planning, that Fashion demands beauty intelligently and happily expressed and that the season encourages slenderness, simplicity, and trimness as emphasized by the new tailored suits and straight-line frocks.

* * *

And if you would be wholly lovely, be womanly in your dress. Wear your clothes with a happy spirit and work always to express a quality of charm that is pleasing, gracious, and individual.

*T*HE straight line is seen in simple and elaborate effect. For instance, the cream crêpe bride's dress shown here features a drape, cream lace sleeves and lengthwise trimming of pearl, the long sleeves and the pearl trimming designed especially to accentuate the straight line.

The bridesmaid wears, as you see, a full, fluffy skirt, but special license is always given to the young, especially bridesmaids, for their dresses should be, if possible, more picturesque than fashionable. In this case, a pale pink slip is worn underneath the dress of cream net which carries bands and bands of pink silk ribbon. And the pink ribbon may be changed, if one desires, to blue, gray, or yellow to harmonize with the color scheme.

The tunic dress of gray lace has a slip of silver satin and a bow of watermelon color taffeta at the left side. Tiny ribbon flowers in pastel tones, with watermelon predominating, ornament the tunic. The hat is of watermelon taffeta trimmed with gray and watermelon ostrich.

The Georgette dress, with its tiered ruffles in straight-line effect and its smart little cape, is of poudre blue. The hat is of brown maline with brown ostrich tips.

The smart wrap is of cowboy color moiré lined with Georgette to match the ribbon trimming of sand color. The open sleeve, the long revers line, and the ribbon trimming all emphasize desirable features.

From Tip to Toe

IF milady would be fashionable and well-dressed this season, she must first look to her corsets. Corsets must allow of an easy waist line, well-controlled hips, and enough freedom to make for suppleness of figure. Even the stouts must wear as limber a corset as possible so that they will in nowise appear to be boarded up, as is so often the case with an overcorseted figure. The elastic corset, which forms a girdle around the waist and comes well down over the hips, is preferred by many, as it allows a straight, graceful hip line.

Brassières of ribbon or banding, 6 or 8 inches wide are very popular, confining the bust just enough and yet not binding the figure around the waist line. A straight-line slip is frequently worn over the corset to serve as corset cover and petticoat. This is made of soft, clingy fabric with few lines and no frills. Very few linings are used so that the dress may fall soft and easy.

THE waist-line finish is slightly more snug than last season and is long in effect. Some of the newest basque effects are rather long and have a shirred skirt or a circular, flaring one.

Dresses are a little shorter than they were last fall, and this is an advantage, especially with summer fabrics, for the skirt may have a little more fulness and thereby achieve a smarter effect. And, after all, the short skirt is often more becoming than the long one.

Some fashion folks say that sleeves must be definitely long or short, but everywhere in the realm of fashion we see contradiction of this. Sleeves seem to be made more than ever to fit in with the entire silhouette of the dress. If long, slender lines are worked for, as in the tailored frock, the sleeves are frequently long. The afternoon dress of soft lace may find them three-quarter length. For young girls and young women, the short sleeve is very much favored, especially the kimono with just a suggestion of a sleeve finished with banding, frill, or lace.

Many of the dresses that are simple in silhouette—two pieces sewed together with an easy sleeve—are developed in soft, luxurious fabrics and trimmed with collar and cuffs that are bouffant and faddish.

The collars are often of the bertha style or plaited as frills, with cuffs to match, and then these are frequently applied with exquisite ribbon—little bows, twisted lines of ribbon, and long tie ends—thus giving the color note and chicness so often desired.

And then, as additional trimming for these plain dresses made of lovely fabrics, there are plaitings of all kinds, plain bands of self- or contrasting material, bands tucked or stitched, bindings, lace, ribbon, and embroidery on panels and overdrapes.

Suits, strictly tailored, having one- or two-piece skirts and short box coats and made of man-tailored fabrics, are ultra smart. They came in with a rush and have met with definite favor.

The tunic dress is another that has crowded its way up to the front and is competing with the straight-line and the coat dress.

Wraps are of novelty cut, some cape-like, but preference is given to the straight, boxy, almost long, semitailored coat.

Apron fronts are very pronounced and are embroidered, tucked, or plaited.

BESIDES the dull, soft-toned fabrics, flat crêpe and Canton crêpe, there is much deference shown to the shiny-surface materials also. Stellar satin, with its very high sheen, is, perhaps, the most popular, but Georgettes, foulards, printed silk crêpes, and moiré all have their part in the fashions of the hour. And of the summer fabrics, ginghams in gorgeous plaids are very appealing and may be developed very attractively in the interesting designs offered. Then there are the lovely cotton crêpes and voiles, the smart, serviceable ratinés, the cotton fabrics of novelty weaves, the plain suitings in imitation of linen, and linen itself.

One sees black satin adorned with organdie, plaited chiffon, exquisite embroideries, laces of all kinds, and ribbon, and again with crêpe and satin. There are two types who can wear black well—the dignified, stately type and the extremely smart type

The colors are quite as new and interesting as the fabrics. There need be no drab-

ness in clothes this season, because even though subdued colors might be desired, there are the lovely grays, the very dull log cabin, which is almost a taupe, the jack rabbit, which is just a little lighter, and cinder. And in the lavenders, there is Eugenie, which is a very clear attractive tone, a wee bit lighter than clover. In the pinks, cherrybloom, cameo, crushed berry, and melon are most favored. In the greens, the lovely soft dryad, which is just a little more gray than almond, and the moss, which has just a cast of yellow, are new. And then comes the lovely jasmine yellow, sometimes called mellow, and the Chinese yellow, just between yellow and orange. In the tans and browns, we have a glorious array, with toast and stucco, Mexico, cowboy, lariat, tan bark, and Piccadilly in the light tones, and autumn and Mandalay in the darker ones. In blue, there are poudre, Daphne, Empire, and Yale, and the old standby, navy, which runs a close second to black but is not quite so popular, black and white combinations leading in smartness.

SHOE-SHOP windows are almost as interesting as jewelers. Shoes are shown so attractively cut and so beautifully ornamented that they seem almost too delicate and ornate for wear. But always, on second looking, one sees a sturdy well-cut Oxford designed for street and service wear, a kid strap in modest design, and neat, black, patent leathers, all suitable for street wear.

Suède is shown in abundance, especially for afternoon wear. White canvas or fabric used to abound in stitching with heavy soles, which bespoke tennis or sports in every line. For this spring and summer time, the shops are showing white and delicately-colored slippers in kid and satin suitable for wear with every flimsy whim of a dress.

Stockings for the lady are quite modest. Modish stockings of open work, embroidery, clocking, and high color, especially for sports wear, are to be seen. But the stockings must be bought to suit the occasion perfectly; and special care must be taken that they match the dress or suit or at least are of an agreeable contrast.

DRESSES with their interesting neck lines, smart ties and ribbon trimmings, make necklaces a little less popular, yet many are seen, especially pearl. Bracelets are in abundance, short sleeves giving them full sway.

Parasols, like fans, are always in evidence for the one who knows the art of carrying them. This year, they are of many colors with beautiful handles, in the main, more or less "tailored" in appearance.

There are short gloves of suède, kid, silk, and fabric, with scalloped or trimmed wristlet cuffs to wear with both long- and short-sleeve dresses; the very long gloves of kid, suède, and silk for the short-sleeve frocks; and the sturdy gauntlets for sports and service wear. The gloves and hose are frequently matched in color, and sometimes the veil joins the other two in a happy trio.

Often, leather trimming is used on the hat or frock to match the purse. The jaunty ribbon or leather fob that hangs from the wee pocket on jacket, blouse, or skirt is often of a color to match the purse. If you have a watch too large for wrist wearing, bring it out and attach it to one of these "up-to-the-minute" fobs.

BAGS are daintier and more exquisite, perhaps, than in many seasons, many of them made of fabric with ribbon or embroidery trimming. The arm purse, like a small treasured book, is covered with beautiful moiré, brocade, or grosgrain, and sometimes has an applied design of embroidery, tapestry, or beading. The shiny, black patent leather purses match the shoes, and the suède purses come in colors and types to harmonize with every costume.

And so with veils. For every hat, there seems to be a veil especially planned. Of sheer mesh, lace, dotted mesh, or ribbon or fabric trimmed, some are quite heavy in texture, others so "cobwebby" that one has to look twice to make sure that a veil is being worn.

Scarfs of fabric are shown in many smart shops. The loveliest and most serviceable ones are of bright color and exquisitely soft texture. Since they can be made of fabric or ribbon at home, every sports hat and suit can, if the wearer chooses, boast a smart scarf, which may help to express brightness, chicness, or individuality, if just the right color or texture of material is chosen. The gardenia bouquet also is a brightener for somber suits and helps to emphasize trimness, which the new suit silhouette demands.

Straight-Line Dress

Straight-line dresses are a delight to see and quite as smart as they are practical. Their simplicity demands, however, that they be made as perfectly as possible and that infinite pains be taken with the little details so that the dress has interest and charm.

The dress illustrated in Model 1 is simplicity itself, yet it does not require much imagination to realize how very attractive and becoming it could be if it were developed in any of the firm silks, such as Canton crêpe or crêpe de Chine, in the soft wools, or in any of the cotton or linen suitings. A frock of silk or cotton ratiné could be made decidedly smart and desirable in this style. Consider, for a moment, how lovely it would be made of poudre blue Canton crêpe with black and white crêpe de Chine trimming, or of mocha color Canton with brown and tan trimmings, or in white with black and white trimmings.

Material and Pattern Requirements.—Excella pattern E1491 is used in developing this dress. Only two scant lengths of material are needed because of the binding at the bottom, which serves as a hem finish. If the figure is large, it may be necessary to plan the cutting so as to piece the sleeves underneath. In many of the ready-to-wear dresses, for economy's sake, the seam is made to come 2 or 3 inches back of the regular sleeve seam and directly under the arm. This, in the crêpes, when pressed open flat, is scarcely visible and often may save a full sleeve length of material.

Construction and Fitting.—In developing this dress, if the material is at all firm, use flat, pressed-open, overcasted seams. In crêpe de Chine, French seams may be used, but they should be pressed very flat to give a smooth, well-tailored effect. After the dress is seamed, put it on to make sure that its proportions are correct. The dress, because of its plainness, should fit easy and not too snug. After the fitting points are considered and

the correct length is determined, apply the vest portion to the center front. This is put on with the plain seam down the revers edges, and the vest portion turned to the right side, where the raw edge is covered by the binding trim of the vest.

This binding is made of two bias pieces of the trimming material. The darker trimming color is put on first and stitched in place as an applied band. The lighter color is made as a milliner's fold and slip-stitched directly above the stitching of the applied band.

The hem of the skirt is finished in the same way as the vest, except that the exact skirt length is first determined, and then the darker band is applied as a binding, the raw edge of the skirt being concealed within the binding band. The milliner's fold is applied directly over the stitching line. This, by the way, is a smart finish for firm wash fabrics or for silks and wools.

For the motif in front, a bias fold of the darker trimming color is used for the oval, while wee bits of the light color are made into a fold to fill the space.

The collar and cuffs are made perfectly plain and stitched and turned right side out; then they are carefully pressed so that no stitching is necessary on the outside.

An essential point in the smartly tailored garments of the season is to achieve smooth, easy lines for collars, cuffs, hems, bands, and all trimmings without any visible machine stitching. To insure perfection with such details, straight, easy stitching, accurate turning, and careful pressing are necessary.

If this dress were developed in wool, welt pockets would be in order, but in Canton crêpe wash pockets serve admirably and require only a milliner's fold of the self-material neatly turned in at the ends as a finish.

A belt ¾ inch wide, made double of the material, extends from side front to side front across the back. The belt must snap at the left-side front or the dress must be left open above and below the waist line at the left side to permit its being slipped over the head.

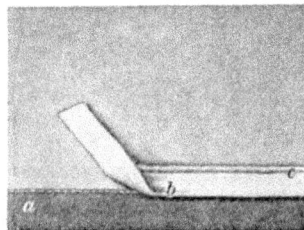

To finish the bottom of the skirt, cut a bias strip of the dark color 1½ inches wide, and apply as a ½-inch binding, as at *a*. Make a milliner's fold of a strip of the light color 1½ inches wide, which, when finished, will be from ⅜ to ½ inch wide, and apply with slip-stitching so that it just covers the stitching, as at *b*. The raw edges are turned inside at *c*.

Embroidery as a Trimming Medium

The Breton shapes, whether straight, curved, or flaring across the front, are maintaining the prestige they have established in hatdom because of the becomingness of the easy rolling brim to so many different types. A truly distinctive type of the Breton is shown in Model 1. The top brim is covered plain with black ciré haircloth, while the facing repeats the color of the dress material. Outlining the rolled edge in a flange effect is a simple embroidery design made with a strand of Coburg braid.

The rather high bowl-shaped crown of the haircloth has its top portion divided from front to back with a 1-inch band of the facing material, which also forms the fitted side crown that shapes up a trifle in the front. A scroll design of the same braid is used on the side crown and across the crown band.

A generous-size cabochon, covered with the crêpe and having a Chinese motif in the center and a scroll around the edge, is applied in the center front as a trim.

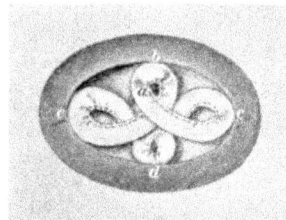

For the oval of the front trimming motif, cut a bias of the darker color 1⅛ inches wide and make into a ⅜-inch tube. Connect the ends with a bias join. Press in oval shape. Make a similar ¼-inch tube of the lighter color. Draw this into position with running stitches, as at *a*. Tack to the oval at *b*, *c*, *d*, and *e*. Slip-stitch the oval to the dress.

Model 1

Variations of Straight-Line Dress

Model 1A.—Simplicity and straight line seem almost synonymous when applied to the season's fashions, and for the woman who wishes to appear more slender than she really is, the fashion is a popular one.

Take, for instance, the sports type of dress illustrated in this model. Novelty-silk, cross-barred fabric is used with trimmings of plain silk and harmonizing texture. The trimming material is arranged to give a straight line down the front of the dress, helping to produce an effect of slenderness and breaking agreeably the width that would result from the cross-barred design. The narrow belt, the long, tight sleeves, and the button trim also are slenderizing features and at the same time give a desirable style emphasis.

McCall pattern 3584 may be used for the dress, the pattern calling for 4¾ yards of 36-inch material with the cape. If contrasting material is used, as shown here, then 2¾ yards of cross-barred material and 2 yards of plain should be purchased. By this plan, the cape is made of the plain material.

Model 1B.—This jaunty, youthful dress is certain to be becoming to a slender figure. Though straight in line, it might prove an unwise selection for a slightly large figure because of the trimming around the waist line.

In this case, the material is gray Roshanara with poudre blue crêpe de Chine trimming. But if one does not want gray, then white with yellow, green, or blue trimmings would make a lovely dress—one that could serve as one's best for summer wear. The dress slips on over the head, and the belt snaps together when the dress is on.

A long plain-waist pattern is essential, but the skirt may be made of two widths of the 40-inch material with the fulness arranged in five plaits on the left side and three on the right. Provide 3½ yards of 40-inch material with ¾ yard of contrasting material for the collar, tie, and waist-line trimming.

Model 1C.—The original of this was developed in yellow-and-white flannel with a white broadcloth band, white loops, and silver buttons, and made a thoroughly attractive straight-line sports dress. If one prefers a wash dress instead, a yellow-and-white checked gingham having a cross-bar of black, with organdie fold, buttons, and loops, would be very effective; or the organdie might be omitted and a bias fold of the gingham used for the trimming band.

In any event, use Excella pattern E1413 and buy 4 yards of 36-inch flannel and ¾ yard of broadcloth, or 4½ yards of 32-inch gingham and ¾ yard of organdie.

Model 1D.—Silk ratiné is the fabric of this dress, and if you haven't seen it, ask for it the next time you are in a shop. It will surprise you in that it does not look like silk, but is as soft as linen, will hang better than cotton, and looks so good in color and quality as to please you thoroughly. As you wear and wash silk ratiné, your satisfaction will be increased and you will come to appreciate it as you do good quality crêpe de Chine or linen.

The dress, in design, has all the smartness of a suit, acquired, as you see, by means of the front waist-line trimming which gives a jacket effect.

McCall pattern 3617 is used for cutting the dress and calls for 3¾ yards of ratiné and ½ yard of crêpe de Chine for cuffs and scarf. Green ratiné with white scarf, or lavender, gray, or any of the season's colors with white trimming would prove attractive and make the dress itself a real asset to any wardrobe.

Model 1E.—That a dress can boast a smart apron tunic and yet maintain a modish slimness of line is evidenced by this model. As pictured, it is made of a fine quality of tan Everfast with plaited inserts and frills of brown organdie.

Choose a straight, simple pattern, such as McCall 3584, to use as a foundation. Then cut a perfectly straight piece, 30 inches wide, for the apron. Put the facing for the scalloped edges on the right side of the apron and stitch through both thicknesses of the material along the line marked for the scallops. Then turn the facing to the wrong side, and leave the edge free. Arrange to use a selvage for this, if possible.

Secure the top of the small pocket to the inside of the apron, and the frill to the outside, with the same binding. Then stitch the bottom and sides of the pocket to the dress proper.

For size 36, 4⅜ yards of Everfast 36 inches wide, and ⅛ yard of organdie are required.

Model 1F.—In this model, we have the smartest of the ginghams—the wide stripe—and when so attractively cut and assembled, a truly distinctive dress results. The original was developed in fine quality gingham having a cream ground with wide stripe of dull blue and tiny stripes of black, with white gingham collar, cuffs, and belt, and black ribbon tie.

If a pearl buckle is available for the belt, use pearl buttons as a side-front trimming; otherwise, organdie buttons may be used. Or glass buttons, which are so attractive and popular and have the virtue of being washable, would produce a novel and decorative effect, especially when sewed on with thread of a color that appears in the material. Then, too, they give such a comfortably cool appearance to a dress on a hot day. Two buttons sewed together will serve as cuff links and be in complete harmony with the rest of the trimming.

Use Excella pattern E1420, which requires 4½ yards of 32-inch gingham with ⅓ yard of plain for collar and cuffs and 1½ yards of ribbon for the tie.

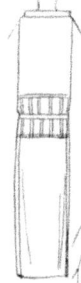

1a

1B

1C

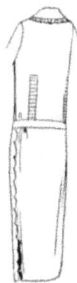
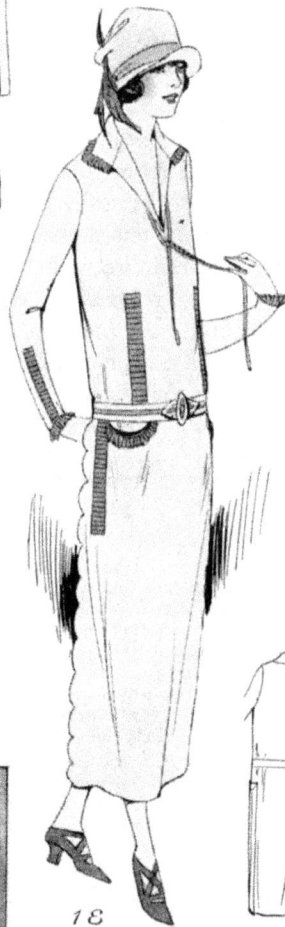

1D

1E

1F

Kimono-Sleeve Dress

The kimono-sleeve dress has always been characterized by its simplicity. But never before has this simplicity seemed so chic, so youthful, so altogether charming as it does in the new mode. This new note, in its individuality, may no doubt be attributed to the fact that it follows the same trig lines as the set-in sleeve dress, and adds withal an artless grace that is the very essence of charm. It conforms nicely to the lines of the figure without emphasizing them. It is loose without being baggy, and trim without being tight.

It allows of much variation in the matter of ornamentation, and a fairly wide choice of materials for its development. Soft materials, and those of delicate texture are the ones most commonly selected, yet linens and ratinés will be found in the group, too, because it includes the sports type of dress as well as the more formal.

The feature of the kimono sleeve which interprets the new mode most faithfully is the ease with which it conforms to the extreme shortness evident in so many of the new sleeves. In most instances, they are not sleeves at all—merely a drop shoulder—and very often without cuffs. There is the other extreme, of course, of the very long, close-fitting sleeve, but this does not belong to the kimono type.

If one regards a dress from the standpoint of comfort, one but calls attention to another point in favor of kimono sleeves. There are no seams to restrict and bind the arm movements. This very looseness insures a coolness in summer clothes which cannot be found in the sheerest dress of the set-in-sleeve variety.

The model shown is made of crêpe de Chine in cowboy, a tone that is a little darker and more golden than tan, yet it is not quite dark enough to be really brown.

The feature that gives distinction to this dress is the wide plaited band of self-material which circles the skirt and breaks the long slim line. To relieve the plain straightness further, three little up-turned tucks radiate soft folds from each side of the simulated low waist line where the sash ends join the dress in the seams.

In keeping with the skirt decoration are the double frills of plaited self-material which make a winsome finish for the very short sleeves. And to make the ensemble even more charming, this bewitching little gown adds a very "different" collar of sheerest cream net, which grows to almost cape-like proportions in the back. Tiny pearl buttons from the neck line to the very point not only add one more point of interest, but give weight and stability to this dainty bit of decoration. The edges of the collar are bound with ribbon in a darker color.

Material and Pattern Requirements.—For the dress itself, two lengths of the crêpe will be required. To give the best effect, the plaited skirt band should have its lengthwise threads running up and down. In measuring for this section, remember that three times the width of the skirt should be provided, plaiting always taking up three times its width. The loose frills at the top and bottom of this are double, the material being turned back the desired width before the plaiting is done. Seams can be hidden under the plaits.

In order to have the sleeve frills, which also are double, run the correct way of the material, extra allowance should be made for them, too.

The double sashes may be cut from the material left at the sides after the dress itself is cut.

For the collar, ⅔ yard of net will be ample allowance. The seam comes in the back under the row of buttons.

The only pattern that will be necessary is a straight slip-like, kimono-sleeve dress pattern. McCall pattern 3583, which comes in both misses' and ladies' sizes, will serve very well.

Construction and Finishing.—After cutting the dress, finish the sash so that the ends may be inserted in the side seams when they are made. Arrange the tucks at the low waist line, and make French seams up the sides of the dress.

Baste and press the plaits in the skirt trimming section, but do not stitch them. The only stitching required is at the top and bottom where the frills are stitched. Tack the upper frill to the skirt every few inches to prevent its falling over. The skirt hem may be made wide and caught in the same stitching that secures the lower edge of the plaiting.

To apply the sleeve frills, join the lower one to the edge of the sleeve, finishing the edges by bringing the sleeve edge over as in a felled seam and turning the edges under. After marking the position for the location of the second frill, turn the right side of it back against the right side of the sleeve and stitch together. Turn the frill down and press it.

The waist-line tucks will be more attractive if they are not pressed.

Unique Version of the Cloche

There is something more than usually attractive in the ensemble of lace, fruit and cloche shape shown in Model 2. This version of the cloche features a higher and broader crown, due to the Directoire influence on fashion this season. Grosgrain moiré yardage in cowboy color is used to fit the brim plain and makes the soft-tip, two-piece crown. Sprays of hand-made silk grapes in variegated colors are appliquéd at intervals on the side crown. A cable cord covered with the same silk forms the stem effect that connects the sprays.

Draped softly around the brim, with about 1 inch dropping off the edge, and veiling the trimming in a standing airy coronet effect that widens out at the sides, is a strip of 8-inch-wide delicate lace in lariat color, a "lighter-than-ever-beige," producing a combination of colors and fabrics that can hardly be excelled.

Model 2

Variations of Kimono-Sleeve Dress

Model 2A.—Fashion is always seeking pleasing contrast, and here it is found both in color and in texture, for this smart dress of soft black satin is supplied with demure collar, cuffs, and pockets of crisp, white embroidered batiste. It is equally attractive with slightly less contrast, when the satin might be brown and the embroidery cream. Buttons of self-material or crystal outline the bound slit at the center front.

The point of design that is different about this dress is its hip yoke, into which the rather full skirt is shirred. Pictorial Review pattern 2058 may be used. To make a pattern for the hip yoke, measure the hips at points corresponding to the top and bottom of the yoke. Cut a strip of paper as long as the greater measurement and as wide as the yoke desired. Fold a few tiny darts equal distances apart in the upper edge until its measurement corresponds with that of the figure. The seam will come on the left side where a placket will be arranged.

For the average figure, 3½ yards of satin will be needed. The collar and cuffs may be purchased ready made and the pockets omitted, or they may all be made from 2 yards of batiste embroidery 5 or 6 inches wide.

Model 2B.—No clothes are smarter than those designed with mannish simplicity, but developed in a truly feminine manner. This model gives supreme expression to that idea. A pattern is scarcely needed, so simple are its lines, yet if one is desired Pictorial Review pattern 1946 may be used.

The material used is white Hebrides cloth, and the straight trimming bands on collar and sleeves may be either blue Hebrides or blue-and-white smocking cloth, an attractive new material of the cotton-crepe family. Black-and-white ratiné may be used for the dress, if desired. The monogram is embroidered in blue to match the other trimmings.

Two lengths of white Hebrides cloth, ¼ yard of blue Hebrides cloth, and one skein of blue embroidery cotton will be needed.

Model 2C.—Fashioned of maize-color voile or pink crêpe de Chine with inserts of filet lace, this dress is equally appropriate for an afternoon party or for church.

It strikes a very charming youthful note in the tucks, which are arranged in yoke effect in both the front and the back of the blouse. The most original detail in the dress is the manner in which the filet lace is used to form the dainty pockets. The side of the lace which is to be the top is bound with the material. Then the pockets are basted in place and hemstitched on with machine hemstitching, which then continues in two rows across the back of the skirt and around to the other pocket. A third row is provided by having the wide hem secured with hemstitching. The inserts in the front and the sleeves are hemstitched in and the material is cut out from under them. If one wishes to add hand-work, the hemstitching may be replaced by fagoting.

Since the skirt is merely two straight widths of the material, the only pattern needed is a kimono-sleeve blouse pattern, such as McCall 3629. The tucking is done before cutting the material.

The blouse closes in the center back with tiny pearl buttons. A narrow belt of self-material circles the waist.

Model 2D.—One of the very popular silks is crêpe satin. Its popularity is due in part to its wearableness and in part to its lovely soft texture. But one of its most attractive characteristics is its ability to form its own trimming by merely combining its satin and crêpe sides. This is one of Dame Fashion's tricks of which she is particularly fond this season. The cape-back feature in dresses of practically every kind is another favorite.

The model shown is especially fortunate in that it combines both of these features. In this instance, the crêpe satin is in Mexico, a new tone of brown that has a decidedly henna cast. The sleeves gather demurely into tiny bands that give them a puffed effect. A long sash of self-material drapes through a ribbon-covered or novelty ornament to the bottom of the skirt, which is formed of bands of the material sewed together in plain seams. The lower band is double.

A pattern will be necessary for the unusual cut of the blouse, Woman's Home Companion pattern 4437 being very similar, and 5 yards of crêpe satin will be needed.

Model 2E.—With all her liking for tunics and flounces, Fashion puts the stamp of her approval on this simple straight-line dress. To indulge her liking for variety, she adds novelty ribbon or narrow crêpe de Chine pipings of green, blue, and tan to a simple affair of brown silk ratiné, and then to relieve the severity of line she tucks little écru lace frills into the front opening and the rather deep armholes. That is all, except to add a few shirrings at the shoulder and to take small tucks to restrain the hip fulness. These tucks are very different from the usual ones for they are made on the wrong side, so that on the right side they look like mere creases in the material. They give a very smart line, indeed.

One might wish to make the model in wash material. In that case, Hebrides cloth with colored bias-tape pipings will fill the need excellently. Or, for a still different effect in silk, one may use silk-and-wool Canton crêpe. Three-quarter length sleeves may be had, if desired.

Two lengths of material will be sufficient for the sleeveless dress, and ½ yard more should be added for the three-quarter length sleeves; 4½ yards of ribbon and 1½ yards of lace will supply the trimming. If bias bands of crêpe de Chine are used, supply ¼ yard of each color. Slightly more banding and less lace are used with the longer sleeves. McCall pattern 3506 will serve as a guide.

2C

2D

2B

2A

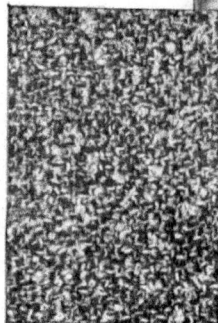

2E

Draping of Kimono-Sleeve Dress

What a multitude of needs the afternoon dress does minister to! It seems one never can have too many. And when they are so easily made as the attractive model here shown, one need not hesitate to add another to an already well-stocked wardrobe.

The material itself may be used for the draping instead of muslin, because of the simplicity of the design. Corn-color Canton crêpe is the material used for this model, though crêpe de Chine would be very attractive, especially in white, with little figures in Chinese effect, embroidered in brilliant Chinese colors in an allover design on the apron tunic.

Draping the Dress.—No lining is used, but a foundation belt is placed in the position desired for the waist line, which is usually several inches below the normal waist line. Pin this belt around the figure with the closing at the left side.

Fold the material lengthwise, as in *a,* and place it on the figure with the folded edge about ¼ inch beyond the center front. This precaution insures against having the dress too small in case the material should slip slightly from its original position during the draping. Pin the material at the shoulder 1 inch from the edge and down the front along the fold, as well as under the arm on the belt.

Cut the material along a thread at the bottom, leaving enough for a hem of the width you desire. Cut the material at the sides at the desired waist line, as in *b,* making about an 8-inch slash and drawing a thread to obtain a straight line. No attempt should be made to cut both thicknesses at the same time, as one might be draped on a slightly different line from the other and the results would not be uniform. Be sure to hold up the material so as to assure making the cut low enough.

With another piece of material, apply the back, as shown in *c,* by repeating the process just described for the front.

Remove both the front and the back from the figure. Then unfold the back piece and lay it across the figure, as in *d,* pinning it to the shoulders. Arrange two small folds at each side near the slash and pin them to the belt, as shown. Next, draw the back skirt corners around to the front, as in *e,* overlapping and pinning them to the belt.

Apply the front of the dress, as in *f,* pinning it at the shoulders 1 inch below the edge and at the waist line at the center front. Lay in two folds directly

To apply the plaiting, place it between the material and a ¾-inch bias binding with all edges even, and stitch ¼ inch from the edge, as at *a.* Turn the free edge over to meet the stitching and baste to the seam, as at *b,* without bringing the stitches through to the part of the binding which will show. Press the whole seam away from the plaiting and blind-stitch the edge, as at *c,* working to get an easy edge that will not draw.

in front of the slash on each side of the front at the low waist line and pin them to the foundation belt.

Draw the corners of the front skirt portion around to the back, as in *g,* and pin them at each side back, just beyond the pinned folds, leaving a 3- or 4-inch end to drape. Mark off the skirt length in the back section.

As shown in *h,* mark off with pins the front skirt section about 12 inches from the floor in the center front, rounding off the corners in an upward line to the selvage. Cut away the surplus material. Pin the front and the back waist sections together over the shoulders, trying to obtain a good line for the drop-shoulder effect. Then, mark the neck, sleeve, and under-arm lines, as shown in *i,* and cut along these lines, allowing generous seams for finishing. Make a slash a short distance down the center back at the neck line.

Prepare two knife-plaited strips 7 inches wide, with one edge hemmed or picoted, and attach the unfinished edge to the drop-shoulder armhole with the seam in line with the under-arm seam of the dress. Prepare another strip of plaiting and attach it to the edge of the front skirt section. Have this 7 inches wide across the center front of the skirt, but gradually narrow it to 4 inches in width when it reaches the selvage in the back.

Apply a beaded motif or other ornament to the waist line at the center back, and extend the trimming band to the side fronts of the waist just far enough to cover the folds at each side.

Finishing the Dress.—To unfasten the dress, arrange for snap fasteners along the top of the front skirt section at the left-side back from the drape to the under-arm seam. Slash an 8-inch placket in the back skirt section at the left side in line with the under-arm seam, which is left open 4 inches for a continuation of the placket. The dress slips over the head.

Bind the neck edge and the short center-back slit with bias strips of self-material, leaving ends which are long enough to tie in a small bow as a closing for the back. The end edges of these ties are turned inside and slip-stitched together so as to make a neat finish.

Finish the joining of the plaiting to the front skirt section and the sleeves with a bias binding applied as shown here.

For a similar effect on a larger figure, none of the front skirt section will drape below the waist line at the back, but the plaited section alone will form sufficient drape to produce a graceful effect.

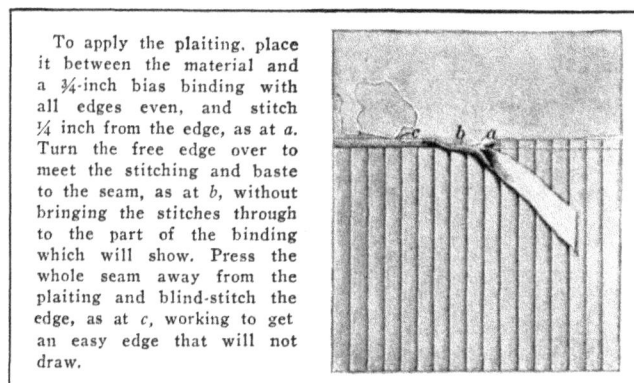

(a)

(b)

(c)

(d)

(e)

(f)

(g)

(h)

(i)

Model 3

Tunic Dress

What an interesting thing the tunic is and how strongly it appeals to the imagination! To recall it as a part of the attire of Roman soldiers, or to bring to mind its association with Greek or with Saxon history, is immediately to surround it with romance. One must recognize that it is a classic in the realm of dress to have been able to survive through the centuries in any form.

Here it is this year—our heritage from the past—with a diversity in cut and trimmings which characterizes it as suitable for street, sports, or semiformal occasions.

Of the dressy type is the winsome gown shown here. In cosmos, or rose orchid voile, with the "airy fairy" touch of hand-made, white, net-footing trimmings, it is a fitting gown for the daintiest maid.

Because the material is sheer and dainty, falling gracefully and easily into soft folds, the tunic chosen is a gathered one, which can be quite full without danger of bulkiness that will detract from its daintiness.

A very youthful touch is added in the hand-run tucks at the shoulders. White voile fashions simple cuffs and a dainty collar for the bateau neck line.

Ostensibly for the sake of giving emphasis to the gown but manifestly to display its own particular charms, lovely satin ribbon of a considerably deeper tone than that of the dress circles the waist and flaunts a capricious bow.

This model is one that lends itself well to development in such materials as Georgette and organdie. And since net is again gaining favor among dainty dress materials, it might even be made entirely of net. Some of the most attractive dresses for semiformal occasions this season are of white net with appliqué trimming in voile or sheer handkerchief linen of one or two dainty colors. The appliqué is applied with blind-stitches. It would be attractive as a substitute for the applied footing decoration of the model as shown.

When the dress is made of organdie, narrow picoted organdie ruffles of the same or a daintily harmonious pastel color would supply the trimming. Or, if desired, embroidery may take its place on any fabric.

Material and Pattern Requirements.—Since voile is so sheer, the very best way to obtain the most pleasing results is to make a costume slip entirely of voile. Then there is not the distinct line of demarcation that would occur if the underskirt were attached to a camisole of different material and color.

Over the costume slip one wears the blouse and tunic, which is really almost a dress in itself.

For the costume slip, 2¾ yards of material will be needed. This should be cut plain with a little fulness over the hips. Pictorial Review pattern 2109, which is recommended for cutting the dress, contains also the pattern for such a slip.

For the blouse and tunic, 3 yards of colored, and ⅓ yard of white voile for the collar and cuffs will be required. The trimming, as shown, requires from 45 to 50 yards of ruffles or footing. This includes the edging for the tunic panels, for the collar and cuffs, and for the floral design.

Construction and Finishing.—Make the costume slip first, allowing for a hem wide enough to come above the edge of the tunic.

The pattern cuts the blouse and tunic in one, but if you desire more width in the tunic, it may be cut wider, gathered, and joined to the blouse.

To produce the slightly bloused effect, various methods have been devised. One way is to use elastic at the waist line. Another is to tack the dress proper to the costume slip. While still a third and, perhaps the most satisfactory method of all, is to replace the tackings with snap fasteners, so that the two may be easily taken apart.

All edges may be picoted. This makes a firm, neat finish which eliminates raw edges and to which the footing may then be whipped with dainty effect. The detail below shows how the footing designs are made.

The French seams used in making the dress should, of course, be very narrow for only through care in details will the completed garment attain its greatest charm.

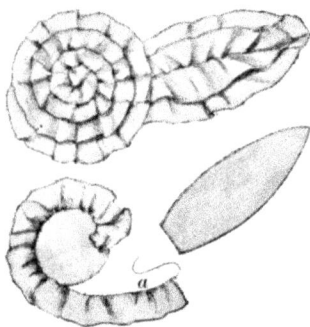

To gather the footing, draw up the thread in one edge, as at *a*. Sew the ruffle to the net foundation, as shown. For each leaf, apply two double rows.

Colorful Body Hats Featured

Body hats of hair, straw, and its kindred fabrics in entirely new weaves, are the feature of the moment. While bangkoks and coconut and yedda straws continue in uninterrupted favor for sports wear, horsehair and the various lacy fiber straws make superb foundations for dressy models. An interesting innovation is shown in Model 4. Horsehair woven like leghorn in cosmos, a rose orchid color, is hand-blocked into a rather high creased crown and a broad-at-the-sides, slightly drooping brim, and has its edge bound with narrow silver ribbon.

Cream-color lace insertion, about 7 inches wide, with an all-over scroll design of varicolored ribbonzine applied by machine, is attached along one edge to the binding and then drawn in a bias drape to the base of the crown, the inner edge being laid in folds on the side crown. As a garniture, a wreath of rose-color oak leaves, their edges tipped with silver, and clusters of silver oak balls encircle the crown.

To prevent lingerie straps from showing with a boat-shaped neck, apply a 3½-inch piece of silk seam binding, tape, or ribbon with ¼-inch hems, as at *a*, to the shoulder seam of the dress as at *b*, leaving the ends loose about ¾ inch. Sew a snap fastener so that when fastened under the lingerie straps the tape will form a circle.

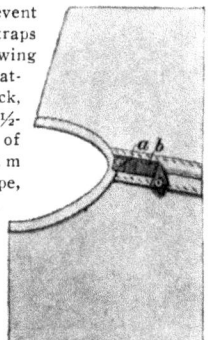

Model 4

Look for a collectible print version at the end of this issue.

Variations of Tunic Dress

Model 4A.—The charm of simplicity is never more pronounced than when expressed through the medium of dotted tissue gingham or soft pink voile. Gray tissue dotted in blue is lovely for this tube-like model with its two straight little apron tunics breaking the long front line. The unique finish chosen for the lower edge of the sleeves consists merely of a band of self-material attached only part way but long enough to band the arm and tie. Ribbon of a blue to match the dots circles the waist line and ties a bow at the front of the dainty lace collar. If made of pink voile, the belt should be of self-material.

For the dress, provide 4½ yards of material and for sash and tie, 3½ yards of ribbon.

Excella pattern E1487 may be adapted by adding the two straight little aprons.

Model 4B.—One of the very newest and most popular tunic effects is produced by a long slip-over type of frock over a longer underskirt.

This model of reseda green Canton crêpe or moiré breaks the plainness of its front by opening from the throat to the normal waist line and tucking in a little picoted frill, which carries out the pleasing contrast introduced by the collar and cuffs in the combination of cream Georgette with self-material. The embroidery at the lower edge of the tunic is green, black, or cream.

The plaited part of the underskirt need not extend above the side opening of the tunic. For this will be needed two and one-half widths of 40-inch material. The other half width, which will be about 20 to 23 inches long and 20 inches wide, may be cut in two, lengthwise, and used for the upper part of the skirt. It should be attached to a long camisole of china silk or sheer cotton.

For the skirt, 2 yards will be sufficient, and for the tunic blouse two lengths will be necessary. The collar, cuffs, and frill will require ¾ yard of Georgette and the embroidery, 10 skeins of silk embroidery thread.

Pictorial Review pattern 2049 is very similar.

Model 4C.—The gay colors of the plaid gingham and the short sleeves of this model give it decided chic. In cut, it is the boyish sports type which has so thoroughly invaded the realm of fashion this season.

A novel cuff makes its debut here. Of white piqué to match the collar, it consists simply of a strip cut about 20 inches long and 3¾ inches wide. It must be double because of the way it turns to reveal its wrong side, as the little sketch at the right shows. The collar is lined with sheer material, such as batiste, rather than made double, as in the cuffs.

If the underskirt is shammed, 5 yards of gingham will suffice, but if it is all of gingham, 6 yards will be needed, together with ¾ yard of 27-inch piqué for the collar and double cuffs. McCall pattern 3607 may be used for the main part of the dress by making it shorter. The under-skirt is straight, except for slight shaping at the hips, and is attached to a long-waisted camisole.

Model 4D.—This model shows a version of the tunic, which is characterized by its dignity, making it adaptable to the more mature figure. At the same time, it is dainty enough to have a very general appeal.

Made of printed crêpe de Chine, it chooses the red of the pattern for the machine hemstitched Georgette crêpe bandings, which emphasize its long front lines and border the lower edge of the tunic. The collar and cuffs are of plaited white organdie.

Pictorial Review pattern 2093 may be used, and 4½ yards of 40-inch crêpe de Chine, ¾ yard of 40-inch Georgette, and ½ yard of organdie should be provided for the average figure.

Model 4E.—Chinese figures on white voile or crêpe de Chine lend a mandarin effect to the tunic dress, which accounts for its being called the Mah Jongg dress.

The one pictured has blue bindings to match the embroidery. The scarf is secured by two corners to the shoulders and left unattached beyond that. The ends and lower edge are bound and the upper edge is finished with a blind-stitched hem or the selvage.

A clever way of introducing width into a skirt without increasing the circumference at the lower edge is done this year by turning a plait about 2 inches deep toward the back at each hip, stitching this down about 7 inches from the top, and then merely pressing it in position to the lower edge, where it is confined by the binding.

For this dress, 3½ yards of white and ¾ yard of blue crêpe de Chine and 6 skeins of embroidery silk will be needed. McCall pattern 3609 is similar.

Model 4F.—Yellow—soft, fresh, dainty, rivaling the first spring flowers in beauty—is a color that Fashion is sanctioning as the season's loveliest offering. It reaches the zenith of its charm in a soft fabric such as voile or Georgette, as in this model, with cream filet lace a very able ally. To give it emphasis by contrast, an ornament of plaited tinsel-edged ribbon is added.

There is a full-length skirt, not too wide, to which are attached two lace-edged tunics. Then a line of insertion, in continuation of that in the vest, extends the full length of the front and has both the skirt and the tunics cut out from beneath it. The material is cut from under the lace in all places, of course, to add to the airy effect.

To develop this model, 6 yards of voile, 1¼ yards of insertion, and 6¼ yards of lace will be needed. If four colors of ribbon are used for the ornament, there should be 1 yard of the color at the top, 28 inches of the next, 20 inches of the next, and 12 inches of that which forms the base. These should be in soft pastel colors.

Pictorial Review pattern 2055 is adaptable.

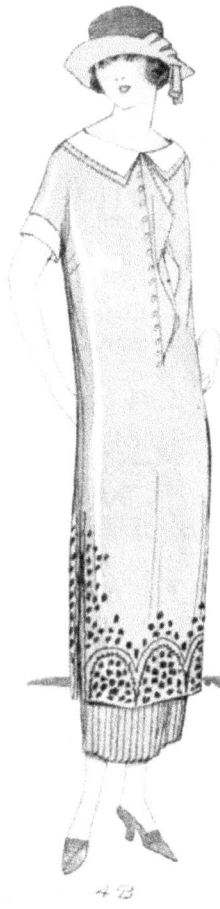

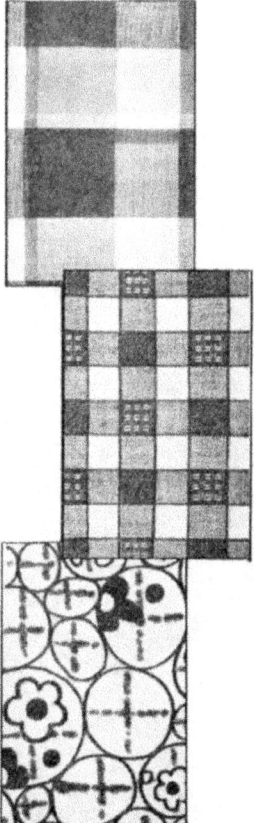

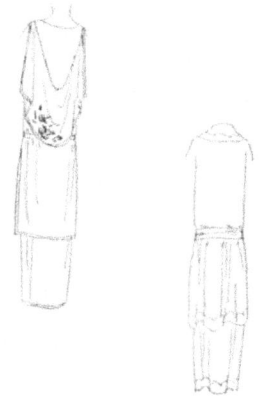

4A

4B

4C

4D

4E

4F

4G

Basque Dress

During many years of favor, basques have gone through an evolutionary process which has left only slight resemblance to the original. But we are quite content with the result since the characteristics retained have included the youthfulness and quaint charm which no other type, no matter how lovely, possesses in such measure. And while changes were in order, a new characteristic was developed—simplicity. In the days of our grandmothers, the basque was the height of a dressmaker's achievement, requiring the skill of long practice to construct it. Now, it requires not even so much as a pattern, as is evident from the directions for draping given below, which, if followed carefully, will result in the delightful little dress shown on the opposite page.

Choosing the Fabric and Color.—This dainty party frock is especially designed for the young miss. The original is made of shot taffeta in blue and tan, with milliner's flowers of turquoise blue at the hips. The waist line tie is of lovely blue-and-gold changeable metallic ribbon. Narrow Val lace edges the skirt and the waist-line frill, and insertion to match provides the neck finish.

Any of the pastel colors of taffeta will be quite as attractive as the one described. And for the ever popular organdie, no more winsome design could be desired. For a dress of washable material, however, the hip draperies should be omitted and the ornamentation concentrated in a dainty nosegay at the center front or the side. For this purpose, hand-made organdie flowers are lovely.

Material Requirements.—For the average slender figure, this model requires 3½ yards of taffeta or organdie, 3 yards of ribbon, 4 yards of Val edging, and 2⅔ yards of Val insertion.

Draping the Basque.—Place a foundation belt at the desired waist line, closing it at the left side. Measure a length of the taffeta from 1 inch beyond the highest shoulder point to the hip and cut along a drawn thread. To determine the width of the material required for the front of the basque, measure the broadest distance across from shoulder to shoulder and add 8 inches. Turn under a 4-inch fold at each side and pin to the figure well up on the shoulders, as in *a* below. Draw the material smoothly over the figure and into folds at the side waist line, and pin it at this point to the foundation belt. Mark the neck line and the trimming line.

Measure the piece for the back in similar fashion to that for the front, turning in 4-inch folds at each side. In pinning the material to the side waist line, do not lay in folds nor draw it too snugly across the back, but keep a straighter effect, as shown in *b*. Pin the back and the front of the bodice together under the arms and mark the desired neck line and trimming line.

Draping the Skirt.—Measure off about 2 yards of material for the skirt and shirr along one lengthwise edge about 3 inches from the selvage and parallel to it. Pin the shirred part into position around the desired waist line, as in *c,* and pin the crosswise edges of the material together down the left side. Puff up the material at each hip and arrange the fulness in position, pinning it to the extended waist.

Cut away the material at the neck line and fit the material smoothly over the shoulders, drawing out the 4-inch fold slightly to produce the drop-shoulder effect. Tie the ribbon around the waist line, adjust the wreaths of roses or other flowers, and arrange for snap fasteners along the left under-arm seam of the bodice and the skirt seam to the bottom of the puffed portion.

Finishing the Dress.—Slip off over the head. Then baste the lace to the edges of the skirt and frill and the insertion to the neck. Draw the waist-line frill down to a point at the center front. Replace all pins and basting with stitching and finish the neck as shown below.

a   *b*   *c*

To turn the corners of the neck finish, slash along a thread diagonally to the edge of the hem, as at *a*. Turn the slashed portion back and fill in the corner with a diamond-shaped piece of the material a trifle larger than the open space. Have the seam inside the hem, as at *b*. Whip the hem in position.

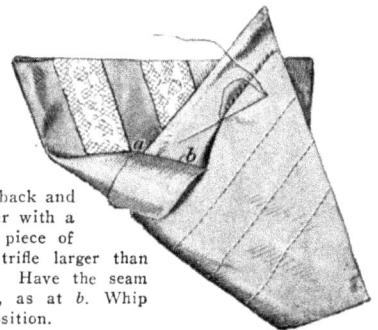

Model 5

Variations of Basque Dress

Model 5A.—The young girl who adores basques but has not indulged in them because of their tendency to make her appear too short, will hail this model with joy. Made of bright organdie, either flame or watermelon in tone, it is a delight to wear or to see. Its trimming is confined to two groups of three lace ruffles each, turning toward the center front. The short sleeves and collarless neck are finished with a bias binding of self-material. A wide hem is always advisable in organdie.

This model may be developed from Excella pattern E1469, and requires 3½ yards of 45-inch organdie and 10⅔ yards of Val lace for the average figure.

Model 5B.—Crisp, permanent-finished organdie in any pastel shade immediately suggests tucks, bound scallops, Val lace, and grosgrain ribbon. When all are combined in one basque model, the most exacting miss cannot fail to be enthusiastic over the result.

To simplify the making, measure for the tucks, mark the creased edge of each, and baste and stitch the Val lace on before turning and stitching the tucks themselves. Mark and cut the scallops before sewing up the skirt seams. These scallops, like the short sleeves and square neck, are bound with bias pieces of the organdie.

To help you in cutting, Pictorial Review pattern 2073 may be used. About 4 yards of 45-inch organdie, 10½ yards of lace, and 3 yards of ribbon will provide the necessary materials.

Model 5C.—Taffeta belongs to spring frocks just as surely as does the basque model belong to the youthful figure. It is indeed a happy dress which serves to bring them all together and adds the winsome quaintness of picoted and plaited frills on the becoming collar and cuffs and the novel triangular pockets. The vest-front effect is merely a part of the basque itself, the collar being applied over it. The simplest method is to finish the neck and collar separately and snap the collar in position. The ends are concealed by a picoted and plaited decoration of self-material, topped by a smart bow of grosgrain ribbon with long ends. The skirt fulness confines itself to the hips by means of a double row of shirring.

About 4 yards of 40-inch taffeta and 1⅔ yards of narrow grosgrain ribbon are required. McCall pattern 3637 may be used.

Model 5D.—Because it may be found in such attractive plaids (which, by the way, are very popular for spring wear in either silk or cotton), gingham is a favorite material for dainty models such as this, in which the old blue-gray-and-white plaid gingham is combined with old blue organdie in plain color.

The popular apron effect is obtained by a perky tie of the organdie, the ends of which join the basque in the side seams just where the organdie side panels come to an abrupt end. The gingham is applied over the organdie on the panels. Its edges are turned in and secured in one of three ways—stitched on the machine, blind-stitched by hand, or machine hemstitched.

To develop this model for the average figure, 3½ yards of gingham and 1¾ yards of organdie will be needed. Pictorial Review pattern 2079 may be used.

Model 5E.—The surplice effect strikes a new note in basque models for the more mature figure. It is accented by the straight collar, which is of the same old blue taffeta as the dress, or of ribbon, if a contrast is desired. The ends of the collar are looped up and caught under two novelty buttons. Val lace edges the organdie cuffs and forms a frill on the inner edge of the collar.

The circular tunic adds grace and makes the model adaptable to a variety of figures. It is bound with self-material and comes within 3 inches of the bottom of the skirt, which is made of percaline with a 12-inch band of the taffeta at the lower edge.

The tunic cuts to best advantage with the warp threads running across, or horizontally. For economy, the 12-inch taffeta band at the bottom of the skirt may be cut in the same way. To make the dress more comfortable, provide additional width in the percaline skirt by means of a 2-inch plait on each hip. The plait is stitched down from the top for about 5 inches. Then it is allowed to hang loose until it reaches the taffeta band, where it is confined by the seam that joins the band and the skirt.

This is a very good model to use for foulard or other soft, figured silk. In this case, both collar and cuffs may be made of plain harmonizing material.

The dress may be made by using McCall pattern 3635. If the band at the bottom of the skirt is cut crosswise and ribbon is used for the collar, 5¾ yards of taffeta will be enough; otherwise, 6½ yards will be necessary. Provide also 1½ yards of percaline, 3¾ yards of lace, and ¼ yard of organdie. If ribbon is used for the collar, provide 2⅓ yards.

About 3½ yards of cording covered with bias taffeta will be necessary for finishing the bottom of the tunic.

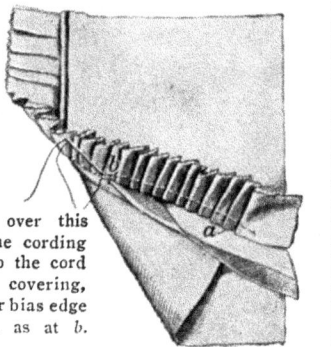

For the cording on Model 5C, cut 1¼-inch bias strips of taffeta. Fold these over the cord with one edge ¾ inch beyond the other and secure with running stitches. Place the cording over the right side of the material with the ¾-inch side even with the edge and baste. Put the 1-inch plaited and picoted frill over this edge with the wider side of the cording extending as at *a*. Sew close to the cord through the material, the cord covering, and the plaiting. Turn the longer bias edge over the plaits and blind-stitch, as at *b*.

5B

5A

5D

5C

5E

Magic Pattern: *A Rucksack Carryall*

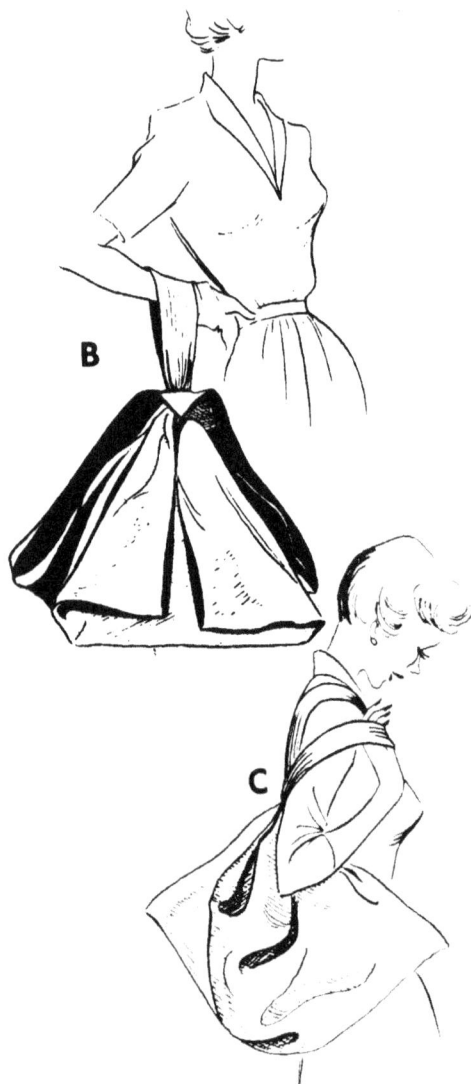

▶▶▶ MAKE ONE of these handy, time-saving carryalls, and every friend who sees this attractive and practical rucksack will want one.

Buy 1⅜ yds. of 36-in. cotton rep, drill, or plain-colored bed ticking.

For the rucksack, tear crosswise of the fabric a perfect square, measured from width. Tear a 13-in. piece from one end of smaller strip for base pocket. Tear off a 19- by 13½-in. strip for over-arm handle. The remaining 4-in. strip may be used for small inside pockets if desired.

Make a ¼-in. turn and then a ⅜-in. turn for a center-stitched hem all around the large square of fabric which forms rucksack. Stitch. For base pocket, make a ¼-in. hem turn on three raw edges of small square. Center this small square on *wrong* side of big square at right angles to corners. Stitch on three turned edges, as broken lines indicate at A. With razor blade cut from firm cardboard or corrugated board a square ½ in. smaller than finished pocket. This slips into bottom pocket when carryall is used as in B. If a soft effect is desired, as in C, the cardboard can be removed.

Faced slash: Mark rucksack square for three 2¼-in. slashes (see D, E, F). Note direction each slash takes in each corner. Cut three 3½-in. strips of twill tape. Lay one of these on right side of slash, as at G, marking ends of slash with pins. Stitch as shown and cut between stitching. Turn tape to wrong side and stitch around the slot twice, as in H, for firmness and neatness.

Make handle by folding strip of fabric crosswise, right side in, 19-in. edges together. Pin. Taper ends so that they measure 4 in., as at I and J, and full width at center (K). Stitch on two sides and across one end. Turn right side out. Turn in raw ends of open end; pin. Place two ends across unslashed corner, as at L, and stitch across handle three or four times to hold securely.

Now for magic! See the attractive form it takes! Lay rucksack right side down. Bring corner with handle toward center, and pull handle through slot D, then slot F, then E. Now open rucksack up again, pack it full, then close it—and you will be delighted with this practical carryall.

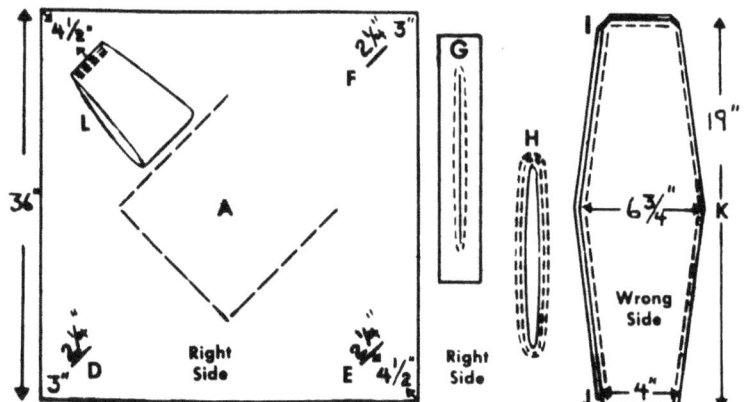

"I've Never Had So Many Pretty Clothes"

"I have more pretty dresses than I ever had at any time in my life. Just think! Six new dresses and two new hats, and last year I really shed tears for want of a decent dress."

THAT'S what the Woman's Institute has done for just one woman. There are thousands of others.

Mrs. E. A. Sherrill, of Texas, says: "The Institute has brought new happiness into our home. My husband is always complimenting me on the things I make." Mrs. Franklin Beecher, of Pennsylvania, is happy because she copied a $135 evening gown for only $22.50. Mrs. J. E. Wise says that "just to hear my daughter referred to as *the best dressed child in town* is worth every cent I paid for my course." A widow writes of making $95 in a few weeks and says the Institute has helped her to keep the family together. A Massachusetts student made $500 in less than three months!

You owe it to yourself—to your family—your husband—to at least find out what this new course can do for you. No longer need you "shed tears for want of a decent dress." If you want pretty clothes, here is the way to get them for a half or a third the usual cost.

What You Learn

How to plan and design becoming garments of all kinds.
How to select, buy and use all kinds of materials.
How to make and apply all kinds of embroidery.
How to make perfect fitting lingerie.
How to renovate, dye and make-over garments.
How to make infants', children's and misses' clothing.
How to make tailored coats, skirts and suits.
How to make pretty evening gowns and wraps.
How to make afternoon coats, suits and dresses.
How to plan and make a bride's entire trousseau.
How to draft patterns.
How to use tissue-paper patterns.
How to use colors harmoniously.
How to dress in taste and style.
How to copy dresses you see in shops, on the street, or in fashion magazines.
How to get a position.
How to go into business as a dressmaker.

WRITE FOR FREE BOOKLET

Write today for handsome, illustrated booklet which tells all about the Woman's Institute, describes the courses in detail, gives names and experiences of successful students, tells how you can not only make all your own clothes, but go into business as a dressmaker, milliner or designer if you desire. Free on request. Mail the coupon or a letter or postal today!

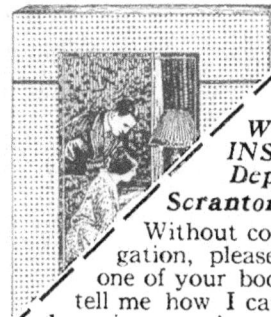

WOMAN'S INSTITUTE
of Domestic Arts & Sciences
Dept. 1-S
Scranton, Penna.

WOMAN'S
INSTITUTE
Dept. 1-S
Scranton, Penna.

Without cost or obligation, please send me one of your booklets and tell me how I can learn at home in spare time the subject which I have checked below—

☐ **Home Dressmaking**
☐ **Professional Dressmaking**
☐ **Millinery**   ☐ **Cooking**

Name ....
(Please specify whether Mrs. or Miss)

Address ....

THE SECRETS OF DISTINCTIVE DRESS

CHAPTER IV

BECOMING DRESS

TRUTHS YOUR MIRROR TELLS—THE PROCESS OF ELIMI-
NATION—LOOK YOUR BEST ALWAYS—CLOTHES FOR
YOUR TYPE.

It takes very brave and sincere friends to be frank with us regarding the things that are becoming to us and those which are not. What woman likes to be told truthfully that a dress she has labored over or paid more money for than she can afford is not becoming? Yet, many times, because we have not given the necessary time and study to the close relation of clothes to our individuality and personality, a dress we have dreamed of, labored over, and spent more for than we possibly should is a distracting failure!

When I was a child, I read a story about a little girl who had never looked in a mirror. Her hair was always tousled, and her dresses were always on awry and always soiled. To tell this little girl about her carelessness of herself had no effect until her teacher gave her a mirror. Then the teacher curled the

Originally published in *The Secrets of Distinctive Dress, 1918*

little girl's hair, washed her face, and tidied her dress, and let her look in the mirror again. This told the child precisely what she should know—that she could be more attractive if she tried.

The value of a mirror in telling us of our shortcomings in dress is something many women do not appreciate. Do not stand before the mirror and comb your hair just to get the locks in place. Stand before it to study the contour of your face—use a triple mirror, if possible—and comb your hair to harmonize with the shape of your face and with your expression.

When you are planning a new dress, put on every dress in your wardrobe and analyze, in front of the mirror, both the good and the bad points of each. In this way you will discern the becoming and the unbecoming points of each dress and so avoid mistakes, for they are mistakes. Anything that interferes with the harmonious costuming of your individual type is a mistake.

It frequently is said that girls in shops and offices dress more becomingly and in better taste than some women who spend three if not ten times as much for their clothes as does the office girl.

Why is this?

The woman of means may be attracted by a new fashion or a new color, and she buys it, regardless of whether or not it is becoming to her individual type.

The office girl cannot afford to buy the first dress she sees. She must select one or possibly two from several hundred, and, seeing the many dresses that she does each day, she, by a process of elimination, finds something that is appropriate for herself and, as a result, is pleasing to her associates.

Put your mirror in a good light, away from any shadows. Then study your face and figure, your eyes, your hair, and your complexion, so that you will know the truth. Mentally resolve that you will not buy anything that interferes with your determination to dress becomingly. This at first may be as hard to practice as a diet for obesity, but it is worth the time and effort it takes if you expect to attain individuality and personal attractiveness.

LOOK YOUR BEST ALWAYS

If long lines in a dress are becoming to you, wear them; do not try to get an "all-ruffles-and-around" frock when you know that ruffles make you look stout and that you lack poise and grace in them.

A much respected woman who holds a prominent position in a large establishment did not for a long time realize the necessity of becoming clothes. Her clothes were selected without any thought, and were rarely appropriate or becoming. One day one of her associates told her she did herself an injustice by the haphazard way she selected her clothes, and suggested that she find a dressmaker who would study her type and design for her dresses that would express her individuality. The wisdom of this advice appealed to her and resulted in a visit to a reliable dressmaker. Later, she appeared at the office in a delightful one-piece blue-serge frock that made her look twenty pounds lighter and ten years younger.

She laughs about it now, and says that before she had been at her desk a half hour, seven of her associates had told her they had never before seen her look so attractive. The foreman of the printery, who had known her and worked with her a number of years, came in and asked:

"Are you going away?"

"Why, no. Why?" she inquired.

"Well, I just had to ask, for I never saw you down here before with your 'Sunday dress' on."

So, you see, our associates do notice; and when we realize how much benefit we derive from being becomingly dressed, then we know that they, too, must appreciate seeing us in harmony with our surroundings.

Not long ago, a business man sent out for three girls who were engaged in the same line of work and who seemed equally capable. He talked to them, and for promotion he selected a girl who wore a very plain but becoming and practical dress. Some one asked him why, and he replied:

"Well, she just seemed to fit into my needs. I know you thought I should choose Miss Blank, but she was too flamboyant. Her hair is too frumpy and she wears too much jewelry to suit me."

"What was wrong with the other girl? She has been here a little longer, you know."

"I don't just know," was the answer, "but the girl I selected will work out, I'm sure of that."

Later in the morning I had an opportunity to see the "other" girl, who was both pretty and capable. One glance told me that a soiled shirtwaist and a piece of gum had kept her from her opportunity.

CLOTHES FOR YOUR TYPE

Every woman and every girl should select costumes in absolute accord with her type; that is, in accord with her mentality, her environment, her duties, her pastimes, her coloring, her height, and her plumpness or thinness.

When the time is at hand to consider selecting, buying, or making clothes, put your whole mind on the problem. Ask yourself: Is it the correct thing for me? Is the color right? Are the lines and the material right for my needs? Does it harmonize with other things I own? No matter whether it is hat, gown, coat, shoes, or purse, this last question should be asked, and then, after it is analyzed and found safe from every other point of view, do not select it unless it suits *your type*.

If you are attractive with buoyancy, express life and personal charm, and have a graceful body, wear clothes that seem to be overly modest, subdued, quiet, simple, and expressive of excellent taste.

A woman who has charm of personality and grace of figure needs but soft, subdued, inconspicuous clothing. By its simplicity and quietness, she may hold fast that charm which is so elusive and so easily covered up or "shooed away" by flamboyant dress.

A beautiful painting expressing life, with soft, exquisite coloring, has its beauty emphasized by a frame so simple that it is not even noticed by you while you "drink in" the beauty of the picture. And so it must be with the charming, vivacious girl or woman. But, remember, it takes more study, more work, more effort, to make a simple frame, a simple gown, beautiful than it does a fussy one, for you can keep on adding and adding to the others until you have a mass of construction. But try to eliminate and you will quickly see that elimination should have been begun the moment the garment was conceived and carried on faithfully throughout the development.

To bring out simplicity of dress successfully means that the process of elimination must be begun before the material is selected. Use only just what is right, and then let each line of the garment express individuality, not conspiracy against the line that joins it.

I recently had occasion to study the types right in my own offices. One day, one of the girls, who is attractive with buoyancy, and who is very close to me in my work, wore a dress that made her look broad-shouldered, short-waisted, and long from the waist line to the skirt hem. I thought about her dress several times, as I really had not been conscious of her clothes before, her personality having always dominated them entirely. Then I decided that the "little blue dress with its indefinite waist line and girlish collar" was the kind of dress for her type.

The next day this girl came to me saying, "Can you spare me a moment just for myself? I want to ask you about a little office dress. I have selected some pictures that I believe you will like."

We looked them over and found the dress that suited her particularly. It seemed just the thing, a beautiful frame for the vivaciousness expressed in her brightly lighted face and buoyant step. It was a modest little frock, to be made of dark-blue smooth-surface cloth, with a white collar that was long in the front and round and sort of "Dutchy" in the back, to give a youthful effect across the shoulders.

Deciding upon that dress set me thinking of each girl who came to my office that day, and I could not resist making mental notes of their costumes.

One girl came, so demure and shy and slight in figure (she is always so meek that I feel I must give her immediate consideration lest she run away). For her, the little blue frock would not do at all. I noticed that her dress was particularly becoming. It was deep red, nearer a burgundy, but just red enough to give a pink flush to a face so fair that it was almost pallid. The dress was simple, but the lines very interesting. I turned back my thought clock just for a moment and remembered that when I first saw her she wore a pretty dark-red sweater that was "different" and decidedly becoming, and I remembered very well just how it was knitted, emphasizing that she realized, as all women should, the importance of individuality in her dress. Even in her sweater she had secured interesting lines that were expressive of her.

The next one to come was one full of life, of vim, and petite in face and figure. To express her type, she needs clothes that are smart, that have "snap" to them. She is able to wear Dame Fashion's most extreme creations, and wear them well. You will be able to picture her better when I tell you that one time, when she was helping to dress a model for a fashion exhibition, one of the manikins put on a smart hat in such a lackadaisical way that it looked positively dowdy. This little "vim" girl walked up to her, and, without even thinking, took hold of the hat, tilted it slightly, brought it down over her forehead, and said:

"To be truly smart, you must always put your hat on 'with a splash'."

A young woman expressing dignity in her manner and dress came into my office next. She was wearing a black soft-silk dress simple in design and having a white collar so spotlessly clean that it seemed to bear out the dignity of the wearer. Her genuine smile and womanliness seemed, if possible, to be over-emphasized by the simplicity of her costume.

Each year that we live, we should grow and develop with experience, and we shall if we are receptive and interested and grateful for the privilege of living. If we are successful, we must acquire poise and outwardly express our intelligence. These two qualities produce dignity, and as we acquire dignity in manner we show it in our dress.

A woman of forty, on the street or in the office, cannot under any circumstances wear the same type of blouses, shoes, and hats that a young girl can. A great many women have a wrong idea about this, and feel that to appear young—and where is the woman who has not this desire?—they must wear youthful clothes. This is a grave mistake.

If you are forty or more, remember that in wearing clothes that are too youthful for you, you lose your background and you have nothing to aid you in concealing the age that your face and figure evidence.

A woman who has been going to business for five years will always display better taste in dress than one who is in her first business year. Why? Because she has learned from experience that she cannot, from a money-and-time point of view, wear frivolous clothes.

My advice to you, no matter what your type may be, is this: Wear nothing that attracts more than your personality, for then the value of *you* would be lost.

One time, under a picture in a magazine, I read this inscription: "It seems so funny to look back at the styles. They are always so misfit after they have gone by."

I thought over these words a considerable time; then I realized that to a very great extent they are true. Clothes are many times put together without definite thought, without regard for type, and when the immediate time of their wearing has passed, they are nothing short of grotesque.

In reasoning this out further, I took from my bookcase several volumes on historic dress and looked over the pictures. Some of the costumes were beautiful. Those which were beautiful would be just as attractive today as they were the day they were worn. I then thought of women whom I knew and whose clothes will live.

"Wear nothing that attracts more than your personality, for then the value of *you* would be lost."

My mind saw a vision of Mary Pickford—Mary Pickford, one of the most successfully dressed artists of this age. I say most successfully, because Mary Pickford makes her clothes express youth in every line—youth that makes her and her work a wonderful triumph.

The pictures in which Mary Pickford's costumes have a prominent part will live for an indefinite time because of the simplicity, quaintness, and charm that is carried out to the minutest detail in every one of them. She never follows a definite fad or fancy, but selects clothes that are becoming to her individuality—to her type—clothes that are in keeping with the parts she plays.

We play a part in every-day life, just as Mary Pickford plays one on the screen; but often we do not realize that we have a part—a part in dressing appropriately and becomingly for everything we do, so that we shall make a picture that is pleasing to all who come in contact with us—a picture that will long remain in the thoughts of our friends.

Artcraft Pictures   *Photo by Hartsook*

MARY PICKFORD
Whose clothes express the charm of youth

Vintage Notions Monthly continues to share the work of Mary Brooks Picken and the Woman's Institute which inspired my book *Vintage Notions*. Although the Institute was founded 100 years ago, the treasure trove of lessons and stories are still relevant today and offer a blueprint for living a contented life.

If you enjoyed this issue of *Vintage Notions Monthly*, visit AmyBarickman.com for more of my curated collection of vintage content including patterns and books for needle and thread, inspiring fabric and textiles & free vintage art every Friday. Be sure to tune in to *Vintage Notions* episodes for a guided tour through my collection of sewing and fashion history, as well as modern projects inspired by my extensive library.

Vintage Notions Monthly, Issue 15 (VN0203)

For wholesale ordering information contact Amy Barickman, LLC at 913.341.5559 or amyb@amybarickman.com, P.O. Box 30238, Kansas City, MO 64112